MADE IN THE SOUTHWEST

MADE IN THE SOUTHWEST

A Shopper's Guide to the Region's Best
Native American, Hispanic, and Western Craft Traditions

by

Laura Morelli

UNIVERSE

PHOTO CREDITS:

Title Page: © Tom Anderson, North American Landscape Images

Front Cover: Rug © Penfield Gallery; Basket, and kachina © West Southwest Gallery; Jewelry © Laura Morelli

Back Cover: Cross © Laura Morelli; Bracelet © West Southwest Gallery; Spur © istockphoto

Pages 11, 12, 15, 17, 18, 20, 23, 24, 27, 28, 34, 36, 38, 40, 44, 50, 53, 65, 69, 78, 80, 81, 97, 99, 103, 104, 106, 109, 111, 114, 115, 117, 121, 122, 124, 125, 126, 137, 139, 141, 144, 149, 153, 156, 157, 160, 162, 163, 164, 187, 188, 190 © Laura Morelli

Pages 6, 8, 82, 94, 119, 167, 170, 172, 173, 183 © Tom Anderson, North American Landscape Images

Pages 57, 58, 132, 179 © West Southwest Gallery

Pages 61, 72 © Canyon Art

Pages 85, 176 © Tex Robin

Page 110 © Garland's Navajo Rugs

Pages 9, 31, 42, 48, 55, 63, 66, 68, 71, 74, 75, 87, 90, 92, 129, 134, 135, 168, 169, 171, 175, 180, 184 © istockphoto

Author photo page 192 © Vincenzo di Cillo

Maps by Lorraine Serra, Chiaro Design

First published in the United States of America in 2006
by UNIVERSE PUBLISHING
A Division of Rizzoli International Publications, Inc.
300 Park Avenue South
New York, NY 10010
www.rizzoliusa.com

© 2005 Laura Morelli

2006 2007 2008 / 10 9 8 7 6 5 4 3 2 1

Distributed in the U.S. trade by Random House, New York

Printed in China

ISBN: 0-7893-1382-0

Library of Congress Cataloging-in-Publication Data

Morelli, Laura.
  Made in the Southwest : a shopper's guide to the region's best Hispanic, Native American, and Western craft traditions / Laura Morelli.
    p. cm.
  ISBN 0-7893-1382-0 (pbk. : alk. paper)
  1. Handicraft--Southwest, New. 2. Artisans--Southwest, New. I. Title.
  TT23.9.M67 2006
  745.0979--dc22
                 2005023693

ACKNOWLEDGMENTS

I am convinced that in our world of mass production and consumption, there is a special place for quality, uniqueness, and individual creativity.

Several years ago I began a quest to find artisans passing on a specific kind of knowledge of the past to the next generation. What I found was that I am not alone in my desire to discover the traditions and stories behind handcrafted treasures. I am grateful to the people who share my passion for the unique, rare, and artisanal.

No matter how timely the topic, however, this story could never have been written without the generous outpouring of assistance across the Southwest from countless arts organizations, craft dealers, and especially, the artisans themselves. Over the course of my research I have had the opportunity to meet some fascinating and generous people, and to spend memorable moments watching the Southwest's most able craftspeople doing what they do best. It is truly a privilege to witness firsthand the care and respect for tradition that artisans of all three traditions—Hispanic, Native American, and Anglo—bring to their work. The more time I spend with artisans around the world, the more I stand in awe of them.

I thank Rizzoli and Universe Publishing for the opportunity to take this journey. Without the steadfast support of Kathleen Jayes, Jennifer Burch, and their staff, this book would not have seen the light of day.

I am ever humbled by my extended family's unswerving enthusiasm for my harebrained projects. In particular, I thank my mother, Beverly Good, for her resourcefulness and for proving herself an outstanding travel companion. Special thanks to Tom Anderson for sharing his stunning photographs and his love of the Southwest.

Most of all, to Mark and Max, thank you for indulging me during the many hours I spent in front of the computer, and for waiting patiently for me finally to open the door to my office and come out to play.

CONTENTS

SPIRITS OF THE PAST

F or centuries newborns of certain Native American tribes were presented with small beaded buckskin bags in the shape of a turtle, for a boy, or a lizard, for a girl. Parents placed their baby's umbilical cord inside the bag, then sewed it closed. In some tribes, the children kept these good-luck amulets for the rest of their lives. In others, a mother might string them onto a belt, and wear them proudly around her hips. Some mothers even counted the bags among the few precious objects they carried with them into the grave.

To the people of the American Southwest, handmade crafts have been much more than just objects. Like the beaded buckskin umbilical cord bags, these hand-made works have been woven into people's lives as a common thread that links one generation to the next. In many ways, the three major cultures of the Southwest—Anglo-American, Hispanic, and Native American—could not be more different from one another. Yet they share in common important artisanal traditions that are inextricably linked to the way people have fashioned their lives in this strange and beautiful land. What's more, the clash and interchange among the three craft traditions produce results both wonderful and surprising.

The southwestern region of the United States—Arizona, New Mexico, and the bordering regions of their neighboring states—claims fame to arguably the richest craft heritage in the country. Certainly no other region of the United States can boast such diversity of handmade goods. From Hispanic crosses exquisitely decorated with straw appliqué to supple leather saddles hand-tooled with intricate floral patterns and weighty Navajo rugs that require months to complete, southwestern arts cannot be beat for their quality, uniqueness, and the inextricable link to the cultural values and historical circumstances of the people in this region.

I want to take you across this vast and changeable land to experience the work of its best artisans—boot makers who craft cowboy boots entirely by hand, *santeros* who carve statues of local saints from the roots of cottonwood trees, jewelers who form silver and turquoise into works of exquisite beauty. My goal is to lead you to the highest-quality, most-authentic craft sources in the region and enhance your appreciation of these three major craft traditions by exploring the cultural forces that have fostered them. This book celebrates those crafts with a long history that still thrive today in homes, workshops, and small studios across the Southwest.

The Southwest boasts the oldest craft traditions in the country. Many Native American tribes of Arizona and New Mexico trace their roots to the Anasazi people who constructed astonishing cliff dwellings long before the great cathedrals of Europe were even conceived. Some of the indigenous craft traditions actively practiced today—pottery and leatherwork, for example—have a history that stretches back more than a millennium.

The Southwest also took in some of the country's first European settlers, Spanish explorers who pushed their way north along the Rio Grande in the 1540s. As they moved into what is now Texas, New Mexico, California, and Arizona, these early settlers brought with them a fascinating mix of craft traditions that perpetuated the memories of both Europeans and the indigenous peoples of Mexico.

Historically, Native American cultures and (especially in colonial times) Hispanic cultures were entirely self-dependent. These earlier cultures of the Southwest relied heavily on craftspeople for their daily needs: baskets to gather the harvest; pots to cook in; plates to eat from; clothing; ceremonial items; and forged iron for hardware, tools, and weapons. Everything they needed to live had to be crafted by hand—wrought iron, clothes and table linens, saddles and horse tack, pottery for food and cooking, religious objects, and more. Therefore, the craft traditions are deep-rooted and long-standing.

When the Anglo-American pioneers moved west on horseback and wagon caravans across the Great Plains and into the Southwest in the mid-1800s, they brought another layer to this already rich mix of craft traditions. They added newfangled consumer goods—from tin cans to manufactured clothing—that would change the face of craft and trade in the region. Over the course of the nineteenth century, many formerly handcrafted goods were supplanted by mass-produced or

at least more commercialized products. The arrival of the Industrial Revolution transformed traditional Hispanic and Native American ways of life and in some cases threatened the livelihood of local artisans. At the same time, Anglos brought important craft traditions of their own, notably leatherworking and metalsmithing, that would play an integral role in cowboy culture and make an indelible stamp on Americans' sense of identity.

One of the most interesting aspects of southwestern artisanship is the dynamic interchange between its three cultures. Sometimes peaceful, sometimes violent, exchanges between Native American, Anglo, and Hispanic cultures have nonetheless resulted in some of the most fascinating craftsmanship in history. Each culture eagerly traded for what the other had, whether glass beads, iron, or coins. They also shared techniques. Native American craftspeople learned metalsmithing from Hispanic newcomers. Hispanic artisans fashioned crosses, boxes, frames, and other objects from the mass-produced tin introduced by Anglo-Americans. And Anglo-American cowboys integrated Hispanic and Native American styles into their outfits, from fringed sleeves to fancy spurs.

Local geography and geology have played a key role in the development of all three craft traditions. The Southwest is mostly arid, which has allowed for the survival of many artifacts that would have not lasted elsewhere—textiles, leather, jewelry, pottery. Geographical isolation forced the early Hispanic settlers of New Mexico to develop specific local styles using the meager materials at hand—ponderosa pine for rustic furniture, dried straw for inlay, scrap metal for modest hardware. The exquisite beauty of many of these items is a testament to the ingenuity and creativity of the artisans themselves.

Strong family and community connections have also fostered the perpetuation of handmade crafts. Trades were most often passed from father to son, mother to daughter, master to apprentice. The combination of oral history and practical, hands-on skill building has formed the core of craftsmanship for many centuries. Today, those connections are looser, but as these are living traditions, it is still possible to watch the torch being passed from one generation to the next.

While Anglos brought a more mechanized society that threatened the longevity of some craft traditions, at the same time they brought connoisseurs and collectors. These important figures buoyed Native American and Hispanic craftspeople who may otherwise have had to close shop after the arrival of mass-produced goods. In the early part of the twentieth century, major aficionados such as Millicent Rogers amassed collections that helped keep alive many of these traditions; they would become invaluable repositories of the Southwest's cultural heritage.

The 1960s and 1970s witnessed a strong grassroots revival of local craft traditions, and the interest and proliferation of them has only increased over the last three decades. This revival of interest in craft ensured that many of these traditions would not only be saved but flourish. In the past three decades, scads of local and national organizations have sprung up to help sustain artisans who choose these careers, and to protect and promote the Southwest's cultural patrimony for future generations.

Today, there is a greater appreciation than ever before for these important historical arts, and much more support for the craftsperson. Regional craft organizations and tribe-owned arts and crafts enterprises now support the work of craftspeople in their own little corners of the world. Individual trade organizations dedicated to pottery, textiles, and other crafts have also helped organize and promote these industries. These grassroots efforts have fueled new enthusiasm into these traditional arts.

Native American organizations undoubtedly have done the most to protect and promote their craftspeople. The Indian Arts and Crafts Association (IACA), the Council for Indigenous Arts and Culture, and the Indian Arts and Crafts Board of the U.S. Department of the Interior help protect the economic viability of the Native American craft industry by upholding legislation against fakes in the marketplace.

Tourism has had a paradoxical effect on the Southwest's craft industry. On the one hand, it has triggered an unfortunate proliferation of tourist traps hawking low-quality, mass-produced wares. Worse, in some cases disreputable businesses sell fake imitations of traditional Native American crafts that are mass-produced overseas. On the other hand, the strong tourism industry in the Southwest has also ensured that its local craft traditions flourish. Greater appreciation for quality handcrafted goods means that there is a healthy trade for these items, and even the highest-priced wares find a loyal audience.

In addition to eager consumers, several other important cultural forces are at work to ensure that southwestern craft traditions endure and proliferate into the next generation. Family traditions still play an important role in Hispanic, Anglo, and Native American crafts. It is encouraging to see so many young people following in the footsteps of their artisan parents and grandparents. Family connections are also still important in the world of craft dealers. Many of the most historical trading posts in rural locales in and around the Indian reservations are still operated by the same families who founded them years ago. And many of the most reputable regional craft dealers are in their second, third, and even fourth generation of ownership.

Today, the handcrafted sector is flourishing like never before, offering people who value uniqueness and tradition great opportunities to appreciate the best of the Southwest. But more than anything else, it is the passion of today's individual artisans that will ensure that these important cultural traditions thrive for years to come.

BUYER'S GUIDE

You've decided to collect a unique piece of the Southwest. Where should you spend your money? The sheer number of stores across the Southwest offering typical local products is enough to boggle the mind. After a while they all may begin to look the same. How do you know you're getting the best value for your money?

WHERE TO BUY

Who you buy from is at least as important as *what* you buy. It's always a good idea to buy directly from the artisan when you can, although direct access is not always possible unless you travel to specific Indian reservations or frequent one of the major annual craft markets. Otherwise, you should always make sure you buy from a reputable dealer such as a museum store or a local business that has earned a reputation over a period of years.

There are few scams to watch out for in the Hispanic craft market. In fact, among the region's best dealers, there are many excellent values in Hispanic southwestern crafts and Latin American imports. Likewise, shopping for Anglo, or Western,

crafts is more or less straightforward as long as you stick to dealers who are tried-and-true in their local markets. Because many of the highest-quality handmade Western goods on the market are antiques, you should always take into consideration the condition of the item you're buying, and find out if the dealer will accept a return or will repair the item if it's damaged.

Shopping for Native American crafts is a bit more complicated, and you should choose where to buy carefully. Unfortunately, a few disreputable dealers have made collecting Native American crafts a tricky business, by offering imitation goods mass-produced in Asia or locally. Whenever possible, buy directly from the artisan on the reservation or pueblo, or from one of the many tribe-run arts and crafts cooperatives. This is your best guarantee of authenticity, and it is usually your best shot at a bargain. Otherwise, stick to Native American arts dealers whose reputation you know. If the business is endorsed by one of the national Indian arts organizations, it's a pretty good sign that their operation is aboveboard.

Trading posts are a popular place to buy Native American crafts. They are ubiquitous in the areas surrounding Native American communities, and they played an important role historically. Some trading posts were set up already in the nineteenth century to cater to the region's burgeoning tourist market, as well as to serve the local Native Americans. Trading posts offered manufactured goods to Native Americans in exchange for their handmade crafts such as blankets and jewelry. The trader became a trusted resource and served as a jack-of-all-trades; there you could do everything from buying groceries and gas to pawning a turquoise necklace or sending a telegram.

In today's still-operational historic trading posts, you will hear native tongues, and see Native Americans sending e-mail, filling out tax forms, cashing checks, and buying provisions. While there are a few truly reputable trading posts and a few that are important historically, be aware that many businesses have capitalized on the name "trading post" without any real connection to the historical ones. So, just because it says "trading post" in the name doesn't mean it's a good place to buy.

Buying from roadside stands can be a gamble unless you are an expert on the item you are buying. Although I have seen people come away with some amazingly good stuff from some roadside vendors, quality, authenticity, and value are inconsistent. Avoid individuals pushing crafts in shopping plazas or tourist-attraction parking lots altogether.

That doesn't mean, though, that you shouldn't buy from someone off the street. Hawking wares in the town square or under the arcade of a city plaza is a long-standing tradition in the Southwest. Spanish settlers along the Rio Grande established outdoor vending areas by about 1700. Today, that tradition continues as artisans sell wares on the sidewalks of Old Town Albuquerque, the Palace of the Governors in Santa Fe, and other locations, and this is a good and fun way to pick up great values on southwestern crafts, as well as hobnob with the artisans themselves.

SAVVY SHOPPER

Quality outweighs quantity when it comes to shopping for crafts, so beware of stores that advertise "the most" or "the cheapest" wares. Heavily discounted merchandise is almost always too good to be true. Many disreputable places leave their "70% off" signs out year-round to lure tourists into paying too much for a lesser-quality item.

Who's a Reputable Dealer?

Don't buy from a dealer who does not:
- have a local or national reputation
- spend time to educate you about what you're buying
- identify the name and location of the craftsperson in writing
- provide a written receipt and/or guarantee of authenticity
- stand by his or her merchandise with a clear return policy

Is It Authentic?

Authenticity can be difficult to judge, even for experts on particular crafts; for example, even people with decades of experience with turquoise say that it's sometimes difficult to tell if and how much a particular stone has been treated. And you'll find veteran Native American rug dealers and connoisseurs examining fibers and weaves with a magnifying glass.

If authenticity is a challenge even for experts, how is the average consumer supposed to make heads or tails of the vast variety of handcrafted goods in the marketplace? The reality is that it is not always straightforward, but a few guidelines should be kept in mind.

Authenticity is a major issue in Native American crafts, since cheap knockoffs and fakes take millions of dollars of revenue from Native American artisans. In 1990, the Indian Arts and Crafts Act made it a felony to sell imitations billed as "authentic" Native American crafts. Organizations such as the Indian Arts and Crafts Association (IACA) and the Indian Arts and Crafts Board of the U.S. Department of the Interior serve as watchdog groups to prosecute violators of the law.

You may see the term "Indian handmade," which indicates that the work has been created entirely by a Native American artisan. "Indian crafted" means that Native American craftsmen have been involved in producing the item, but not necessarily designing it. A few craftspeople have developed hallmarks or trademarks to distinguish their work, which can be helpful in authenticating a piece.

If you are buying a work of exceptionally high value or a high-priced antique, it's a good idea to have the work examined by an appraiser certified by the American Society of Appraisers. As always, it's important to buy from a reputable source, including museum shops, artisan cooperatives, well-established businesses, or the artisans themselves.

HOW MUCH SHOULD I PAY?

How much you should pay depends on the particular item that catches your fancy. Guidelines for prices on specific items are provided in Part II and in sidebars throughout this book.

In general, of the three craft traditions I feel that Hispanic handmade wares are the best value for the money. Even at the higher-end craft dealers and galleries, you can often buy excellent-quality Hispanic handmade wares at a fair price. Likewise, it is possible to find good deals on handmade Western goods, even antiques.

If it's your first time experiencing Native American crafts of the Southwest, you may be surprised at the high prices they command. Many of the highest quality Native American crafts are in great demand among collectors, which has driven up prices and put them out of reach for many consumers. When it comes to Native American crafts, if the price seems too good to be true, it probably is. On the other hand, if you can afford the authentic, quality pieces, this is the best place to locate some of the world's most culturally significant and rare handmade goods.

HOW TO USE
THIS BOOK

This book is divided into two parts. Part I is an armchair-traveler's guide to the major craft traditions of the Hispanic, Native American, and Anglo cultures of the Southwest, highlighting what makes them unique. Sidebars provide specific additional information. These include:

· CHEAT SHEET: a quick reference to help you weed through complex categories of crafts, such as Native American jewelry or textiles
· CREAM OF THE CROP: personal favorite places to shop for specific crafts
· THE REAL DEAL: information about authenticity
· SAVVY SHOPPER: information to help gauge price and value for each craft

Whether you're an avid collector, connoisseur, or curious traveler, I hope you'll find something new and interesting in this section.

The listings section in Part II divides the Southwest by state, with towns and individual enterprises listed alphabetically. Each section opens with a brief narrative portrait of the state's craft traditions, and the historical context for craft production there. Each listing provides the current address, phone number, and Website, if applicable, to the best of my ability at the time of this writing. Obviously these are always subject to change. Many of the businesses listed in this book have Websites, and I have included them whenever possible. You may find it useful to browse these sites in planning your trip, purchasing goods, or communicating with craftspeople and shop owners after you return home.

With the goal of making this book as useful as possible, I have grouped craft production into major categories and highlighted the most popular destinations of today's tourists—Santa Fe, Phoenix, the Four Corners region, and other areas. However, I have also included some interesting sources for crafts that merit a detour off the beaten path.

In selecting the artisans and retail outlets listed in this book, I used several criteria. First, the production of their goods must be achieved primarily by hand. In fact, many of the works you'll find by visiting places listed in this book are crafted exclusively using handmade, traditional techniques. Secondly, I focus on crafts that represent major, long-standing historical traditions, such as Navajo weaving, Hispanic santos, or Western spurs. The artisans creating these crafts are important purveyors of the Southwest's cultural patrimony and should be applauded for their efforts.

Every nook and cranny of the Southwest boasts excellent craftspeople of all stripes. It would be impossible to include them all; to do so would turn this book into a multivolume, yellow-pages-style directory, which is not my intention. There are so many wonderful individual craftspeople in the Southwest; to single out some would be an injustice to the rest. I have avoided digressing into biographical sketches or highlighting the work of particular artisans in favor of offering a balanced historical and practical bird's-eye view of southwestern craftsmanship. There are many helpful biographies and magazine articles on particular individuals that give the proper focus these superb craftspeople deserve.

Finally, I have included a Calendar of Southwestern Craft Festivals and Events that will guide you to some of the region's most fun and fascinating recurring festivals, where you might find great deals on unique crafts and get a chance to chat with the craftspeople.

I am not affiliated with any of the artisans or retailers listed in the book, and I do not endorse any one in particular; however, I have highlighted my favorite places to shop in sidebars throughout the book with stars next to their names. I have done my best to provide an evenhanded approach that I hope will enhance your enjoyment of the Southwest and its incomparable craftsmanship.

Throughout this book I offer suggestions for finding the highest-quality, most authentic examples of traditional southwestern crafts. If you find something that's not listed in this book and you love it, by all means buy it. Shopping in the Southwest is all about discovering things that are meaningful and pleasurable to you personally, and I hope you find objects that bring you satisfaction and happy memories of this distinctive region.

Please share with me your experience using this book, and about the people, places, and treasures you discover in the Southwest. Visit me on my Website, at www.lauramorelli.com, or drop me a line at laura@lauramorelli.com.

Until then, happy reading, and happy shopping!

PART I

THE TRADITIONS

HISPANIC CRAFTS

The craft traditions of the Hispanic Southwest represent a fascinating paradox of Old World values and New World customs, lofty idealism and practical necessity, organized religion and individual devotion, Catholic orthodoxy and homegrown convention.

Over the course of the sixteenth century, European and native Mexican settlers moved north from central Mexico up the Rio Grande into what is now New Mexico. These caravans consisted of an unlikely mix of Franciscan missionaries from Spain and Portugal, lay brothers, silver and gold prospectors, farmers and shepherds, thousands of sheep and other livestock—and, of course, craftspeople. Artisans including metalworkers, iron smiths, carpenters, and weavers were considered a critical force in establishing a new life in the new land. It would have been unthinkable to travel without them.

These early adventurers loaded their wagons and pack animals with precious objects from "back home"—altar panels and other liturgical objects, silver utensils, metal tools, blankets, and objects for trading with the native populations. Moving northward, they lay claim to territories along the Rio Grande, and over the course of the next century, they spread east and west to colonize a huge swath of land that included parcels of present-day California, Arizona, New Mexico, Colorado, and Kansas.

These pioneering settlers had to be entirely self-sufficient, from gathering food to collecting water and building wagons, tools, weapons, agricultural implements, and whatever else they needed to eke out a living and defend themselves from potentially unfriendly Native Americans, who did not necessarily welcome these outsiders. Many pueblo residents rebelled against the Hispanic settlers, though most uprisings were localized and haphazard. The pueblo revolt of 1680, a more coordinated effort by Native Americans from many tribes, drove Hispanic settlers south to El Paso and Mexico. In 1692, when Diego de Vargas reestablished the Spanish presence in what is now New Mexico, Hispanic communities with artisans of many trades flourished again.

In these resettled Hispanic communities of the 1680s to about 1850, craft production fell into two categories: religious arts in the service of the church or private devotion, and objects to serve the needs of daily life—dishes and pots, tools and hardware, leather goods, rugs, blankets, and clothing. To a certain extent, the visual

vocabulary of these crafts was that of the Spanish colonial examples they knew from home: fancy Spanish colonial furniture, ornate silverware, indigenous rugs. Culturally and geographically isolated in the new lands, these settlers adapted this visual vocabulary into a distinctive local style—rustic, understated, and remarkably elegant considering the limited raw materials at their disposal; for example, furniture makers harvested ponderosa pines from the local forests of New Mexico, and onto rustic chests, benches, and cabinets they incised artistic motifs with a Spanish flair.

This cultural blending is evident throughout the history of Hispanic craftsmanship of the Southwest, as these early artisans were influenced not only by their Spanish heritage but also by the new environment around them; for example, they may have learned how to carve the dried roots of the cottonwood tree from their Native American neighbors. In some cases, Hispanic religious statues—*bultos*—even bear a striking resemblance to Hopi katsina dolls. Franciscan priests commissioned some of the most exemplary Spanish-style mission churches in the heart of Native American pueblos. The result of this multicultural blending are craft traditions that are utterly distinctive.

Some craft traditions—like furniture making—evolved in large measure based on locally available materials. Unable to achieve the ornate baroque lines of Spanish colonial furniture with the locally available brittle pine, early Hispanic artisans in New Mexico adapted these visual forms to create their own distinctive rustic style. They flexed their creativity to craft beautiful objects from the sparse natural resources and limited selection of woods at their disposal. Exquisite examples of straw work on crosses and other religious works are the perfect example of this ingenuity in craftsmanship. Lacking raw silver and gold, they learned to fashion precious-seeming objects of pewter and tin.

When Anglo-American settlers pushed west into New Mexico in the mid-1800s, these now well-developed local Hispanic craft industries faced a new challenge. The novelty and availability of commercial goods via the Santa Fe Trail changed the economic landscape of trade in New Mexico. And the arrival of "Anglos"—Protestant East Coast settlers of English and Northern European heritage—brought new cultural and religious forces to the region. By the time the railroad arrived in the 1870s, bringing with it even more Easterners and more commercial goods, many of the handcrafted cottage industries fell into decline.

From the 1920s to the 1950s, many Hispanics tried to "blend in" to what must have seemed like a more progressive Anglo culture rather than follow in their parents' and grandparents' footsteps as purveyors of old-fashioned trades. During this time many of the traditional craft industries waned. Fewer weavers, *santeros,* metalsmiths, and furniture makers were passing on their trades to the younger generation. While Anglo collectors and tourists snapped up Native American crafts with a new vigor, traditional Hispanic crafts remained less popular.

Luckily a handful of Anglo collectors had already begun amassing collections of traditional Hispanic arts. There were also a few coordinated efforts to sustain the local craft traditions. In the 1920s, a colony of Anglo writers and artists in Santa Fe founded the Society for the Revival of Spanish Colonial Arts, later the Spanish Colonial Arts Society. This group helped bring the works of artisans in many of New Mexico's Hispanic communities into a more consumer- and tourist-oriented marketplace, and it also garnered greater visibility and appreciation for their work.

From the late 1950s through the 1970s, a revival of traditional Hispanic crafts gained momentum across the Southwest. Santa Fe's Spanish Market, the premier annual event for Hispanic crafts, was established in 1971 and has continued to grow every year. In the 1970s, regional museums began collecting Hispanic objects and mounting significant exhibitions that have only increased in number and importance to the present day. The Museum of International Folk Art, also in Santa Fe, launched a Hispanic Heritage Wing in the late 1980s, displaying one of the country's most significant collections of Hispanic crafts.

Today's Hispanic artisans are carrying on the traditions of their ancestors with a particular focus on authentically replicating the forms, techniques, and spirit of the past. In addition, many artisans are moving in new directions, still respecting the past but innovating with more contemporary ideas and designs. This represents the most significant development in Hispanic crafts for some hundred years. With the rapidly growing Hispanic population of the United States, this trend can only continue.

New Mexico, especially the areas on either side of the Rio Grande, still boasts arguably the richest Hispanic craft tradition in the country. More recently, southern California and West Texas have become a major force in Hispanic objects *hecho por mano*.

BEST PLACES TO SHOP FOR HISPANIC CRAFTS IN THE SOUTHWEST

Old Town Albuquerque

Old Town San Diego

Santa Fe's Museum Hill

Tucson's Fourth Avenue

DAY OF THE DEAD CRAFTS

H uge skulls dart and weave overhead, borne aloft by people wearing skeleton masks and dancing through the streets in a boisterous procession. Thousands of candles flicker before makeshift altars on the sidewalks, and streamers zigzag through the black sky. The sound of drums and flutes fills the air.

In a ritual that seems to thumb its nose at death, the Day of the Dead, or *el Día de los Muertos*, is the time set aside to bring the living and the dead together in a raucous celebration. Traditionally, families honor their deceased relatives with a colorful display of music, dance, food, and craft. During this movable feast people start their celebrations at shrines they have made in their homes, then move into the streets, and finally make their way to lively and bittersweet celebrations in local cemeteries. The Day of the Dead has spawned rich craft traditions that unleash the creativity of Mexican-American artisans each year.

Of Mexican origin, this carnival of the dead likely originated with the ancient Aztecs, who, like other Meso-American cultures, collected real skulls as trophies and believed that the dead returned to visit the living each year. Originally it was celebrated during the month of August.

The Day of the Dead rituals baffled and revolted some Spanish conquistadors when they arrived in Mexico in the 1500s, and they tried to stamp them out as a backward, pagan sacrilege. Unsuccessful, they finally moved the celebration to the last day of October and first two days of November, to correspond with All Saints' Day and All Souls' Day on the Roman Catholic calendar. It is still practiced at that time today, especially in towns with large Mexican-American populations.

The Day of the Dead is celebrated differently in different places across North, Central, and South America, but common threads include preparing special meals (often the favorite of a deceased relative); gathering in local cemeteries at family burial plots; displaying colorful, often handcrafted decorations and adornments; and sometimes setting off fireworks. In the Southwest, many Hispanic residents build special altars in their homes with flowers, candles, santos, and other objects; each item is an offering, or *ofrenda*, to please dead relatives. Many times furniture is removed from a room so that an elaborate display can be crafted. Special foods like "death bread" (*pan de muerto*) and skulls made of sugar, chocolate, and marzipan are prepared only at this time of year.

Handcrafted goods have long played a central role in Day of the Dead celebrations. Amateur artisans craft home altar decorations including paper flowers, sugar skulls, and images of skeletons painted on wood or glass. Some professional Hispanic artisans focus their work on Day of the Dead decorations. Common subjects include statues of wood, ceramic, or papier-mâché, representing a familiar cast of characters. Doña Sebastiana—an allegorical figure portrayed as a skeletal lady riding in a cart—is one of the more loved figures, affectionately nicknamed "Skinny" (*la Flaca*) or "Bony" (*la Huesuda*).

Skeleton figurines (*calacas*) portray the dead enjoying an active and pleasant afterlife not too different from life on earth—they play music, get married, dance, ride in cars, even smoke cigarettes and chat on cell phones. Many are lighthearted, comical portraits of people involved in activities of everyday life—musicians, waiters, priests, and brides and grooms. Many are placed inside boxes, or *nichos*, that provide a miniature diorama in which the drama of life and death is played out in charming and often humorous scenes.

More recently the theme of death and the skeleton has infiltrated many other crafts in the Hispanic Southwest. Images of *muertos* appear on hand-painted cupboards or chairs, and you can even buy entire sets of ceramic tableware decorated with skeletal revelers.

THE REAL DEAL

Because of the ephemeral nature of Day of the Dead crafts—many are re-created year after year—it is difficult to find antique pieces, but contemporary ones abound.

CREAM OF THE CROP

Hispaniae in Albuquerque (page 140), Artes de Mexico in San Diego (page 125), or La Hormiga Blanca in Tucson (page 115) are all excellent bets for adding to your collection of Day of the Dead crafts. Todos Santos Chocolatier and Confectioner in Santa Fe (page 154) can whip up an edible version to satisfy all your senses.

SAVVY SHOPPER

In general, Day of the Dead crafts are among the more affordable of the Southwest. For less than $100 you can pick up two or three interesting pieces for a starter collection.

FURNITURE

S panish styles have made a lasting impression on handcrafted furniture of the Southwest. During the Spanish colonial period, the modes of sixteenth-century Spanish furniture—ornate lines and incised decoration that commonly included shells, swags, and birds—were borrowed and adapted by the Southwest's furniture craftsmen. Those motifs persist to the present day.

But colonial craftsmen in New Mexico borrowed more than a stylistic vocabulary from their Spanish and Portuguese ancestors. Historians believe that these settlers also borrowed the system of craft guilds that were a holdover from the Old World. To this day, many Hispanic furniture enterprises are family affairs.

The only materials available to furniture craftsmen in the Southwest before the nineteenth century were the great ponderosa pines and junipers that filled the region's forested areas. The brittle quality of these woods—they tend to crack along the grain—meant that carpenters had to stick to straight lines and avoid the ornate baroque decoration that were the mode in Spain and Mexico throughout the late 1600s and 1700s. Early on, artisans were concerned with function over form. Before the arrival of more advanced tools, toward the late 1800s, furniture artisans used basic tools like the saw, adz, and chisel to carve rustic designs in low relief. Common designs were based on flora and fauna—shells, lions, fruits, and plants—which were more understated versions of Spanish baroque styles. Local metalsmiths used the limited iron they had to craft modest iron hinges and locks to complete the designs.

By today's standards the furniture in colonial Hispanic homes was sparse, limited to a few important pieces for storing household implements, clothing, and textiles. The earliest surviving furniture from colonial New Mexico shares much in common with furniture of that era in Mexico and Spain. It relied mostly on furniture that was pushed back against the wall—cupboards, chests, oversize storage boxes, benches, armchairs, and side tables. Many of the most common pieces—chests, or *cajas*—made up part of women's dowries.

When Anglo-American influences began to pervade Hispanic communities in the second half of the nineteenth century, local furniture craftsmen adapted and interpreted the more classical federal styles into their artistic vocabularies. "Anglos" also brought with them the latest tools for woodworking, including jigsaws, opening greater possibilities of decoration for local craftsmen. Sawmills brought milled lumber to the region for the first time. The result was a fascinating mix of traditional Spanish forms and other styles—including Victorian and Romanesque revival—that exemplified the multicultural currents of the Southwest.

Those in search of traditional Hispanic furniture should look for classic pieces made of pine or juniper—a caja, side table, armchair, or cupboard. Craftsmen carrying on the traditional techniques still use the mortise-and-tenon or dovetail joinery to fit the pieces together.

Today, even with modern furniture-making technology, rustic styles persist, seemingly ingrained in the spirit of the Southwest. It is remarkable that many of today's furniture craftsmen still operate family workshops set up similarly to the guild system of the past.

THE REAL DEAL

Many of the Southwest's best furniture makers jump at the chance to design custom pieces. Just ask!

CREAM OF THE CROP

Tucson's Morning Star Antiques (page 115) and Rústica (page 115) are great choices for authentic handmade furniture in the Hispanic tradition.

SAVVY SHOPPER

While contemporary furniture can be picked up at relatively affordable prices, collectors pay thousands of dollars for quality Hispanic chests and benches made before 1950. Some pieces of authentic Spanish colonial furniture sell for five figures.

SANTOS

S antos is a general term that encompasses several categories of Hispanic religious art across the Southwest, including panel paintings, carved statues, and altarpieces. Panel paintings (*retablos*) and freestanding carved figures of Christ, Mary, saints, and other figures (*bultos*) represent a huge body of local craft production, especially in New Mexico, where the tradition is richest. In my view, santos are among the most compelling traditional crafts of the Hispanic Southwest.

Santos rely on Mexican prototypes, which ultimately traced their roots to southern Europe, especially Baroque Spain. However, New Mexican artisans adapted santos to their own needs and also developed their own subject matter and styles. The figures are linear and characterized by simplicity—they are iconic rather than narrative. Uncluttered, they rely on a limited color scheme. Displayed prominently in churches and private devotional spaces, they exude a simple, rustic beauty and emotional power.

Early colonists moving north from Mexico brought familiar liturgical as well as personal devotional objects with them; caravan inventories include bultos on the lists brought from Mexico. They also began to make their own statues and panels to satisfy demand in the new land. The santos that grew to represent a huge craft phenomenon, especially in New Mexico and southwestern Colorado, developed out of the isolation of these groups.

Many santos were destined to serve the needs of local churches or the meeting places of lay brotherhoods (*morades*). Elaborate altar screens (*reredos*) were constructed in an architectural framework, inset with painted panels featuring saints. This was the most common form of church decoration in preindustrial New Mexico, and required the work of skilled wood-carvers and painters.

Increasingly over the nineteenth century, santos were used in homes in private shrines. One of the most enduring features of the Hispanic home were altars set up for this purpose, usually in bedrooms or dining and living spaces, with a santo as well as flowers, prayer cards, candles, and other images. Santos often played the starring role in these domestic devotional spaces, where they were used as "visual aids" to direct in the person's prayers and supplications, as they could petition their saint for healing, faith, courage, or other favors. Today, altars remain an important part of many Hispanic homes.

The narrow range of subjects of southwestern santos include Mary, saints, and more than anything else, the cross, crucifixion, and passion of Christ. The Brotherhood of Our Father Jesus Nazarene, a confraternity composed of pious laymen and laywomen, constituted a powerful force in the Hispanic community through the early twentieth century. Many santos were crafted for use in their feast day celebrations and penitential processions.

Traditionally in the Southwest, santeros, the makers of santos, started with dried and seasoned roots from the cottonwood or pine tree. Some historians believe that the early santeros followed Native Americans in this regard. As it grows along waterways, the cottonwood tree is revered in many Native American cultures and has been used in Native American carvings—especially for katsina dolls—since time immemorial.

The santero used a variety of metal tools to craft the final product; originally local metalsmiths made them, but today's santeros often use modern woodworking tools. At first, pigments were created from locally available minerals and plants, including colored clays, vegetable dyes, and iron oxides. Oil paints were sometimes available. Later, commercial house paints were used.

Bultos—the freestanding statues—were roughed into sections of the body, arms, head, and sometimes legs using an ax, adz, or chisels and various kinds of knives, then smoothed with sandstone. From there, the santero connected the body parts with wooden dowels. As was the tradition in Spain and later Mexico, the wooden form was covered in gesso, a gelatinous material extracted from boiled-down animal tissues (hooves, hides, intestines, cartilage, tendons). Brightly colored cloth was also sometimes covered in gesso and adhered to the wooden body. Once dry, the santero painted the details of faces and costumes. Finally, a layer of varnish was brushed over the entire work.

Retablos (from the Latin *retro tabula* or "behind the altar") were similarly roughed out using an adz on slabs of ponderosa pine, then were coated with gesso. From there, the panel served as a blank canvas for painted decoration and a final coat of varnish to impart a slick, glossy finish. Originally these varnishes were created from pine sap, but today most santeros use commercial products.

The influx of Anglo culture in the second half of the nineteenth century precipitated a sharp decline in the production of santos. Commercialization and the railroad meant that churches and individuals could purchase inexpensive plaster casts and lithographs with religious subjects. The Brotherhood in particular resisted the modernizing influence of the American newcomers, with their foreign Protestant ways and view of santos as artifacts of an outdated and backward society. Hispanic young people had little interest in following in their parents' footsteps and sought instead to conform to what they viewed as mainstream American life, especially during the 1950s. The 1970s witnessed a revival of interest in santos, and

today the numbers of active santeros in the Southwest continues to grow to sustain this important tradition.

Today's best santeros rely on traditional techniques and materials, though many use modern electrical tools for the basic woodwork. It is often a family affair, with parents passing down the old techniques to their children and grandchildren. The efforts of a handful of santero/scholars have helped to fuel the tradition and ensure that the historical methods are passed to the next generation.

THE REAL DEAL

Authentic bultos should be pieced together with dowels, not glue. Originally this made it easier to dress the holy figure for religious processions or feast days, since the limbs could be removed and replaced easily.

CREAM OF THE CROP

For good value on authentic santos, head to Albuquerque's Old Town. His-paniae (page 140) offers a nice selection of contemporary works, and Saints & Martyrs (page 140) often carries unusual or antique examples that are museum-quality. Several museums—including the Taylor Museum in Col-orado Springs (page 130), the Albuquerque Museum (page 139), and the Museum of Spanish Colonial Art in Santa Fe (page 154)—also hold impressive collections of santos for the serious collector, connoisseur, or curious tourist to examine.

SAVVY SHOPPER

Many contemporary New Mexican santos can be had for $50 to $500, making them a good value considering their uniqueness. Antique or unusual examples command higher prices.

MILAGROS, EX-VOTOS, AND OTHER DEVOTIONAL ARTS

In addition to santos, throughout the Southwest craftspeople have fashioned many other objects in the service of collective and individual devotion. *Milagros*, *relicarios*, and ex-votos have played an important role in Hispanic devotional practices and craft production across the region.

Milagros (miracles) are tiny metal representations of body parts and humans, animals, and objects. Milagros are one type of ex-voto—an object offered in supplication to a particular holy figure. The devout offered milagros at pilgrimage churches, either to give thanks for an answered prayer or to lobby a particular saint for a miracle. To heal a broken leg you might offer a milagro fashioned as a tiny leg; for a bountiful harvest you might offer one in the shape of a sheaf of wheat.

In the past, people either commissioned a smith to make the particular milagro they wanted or they could purchase one from a vendor of religious items. Some shrines became so plastered with them that the church would resell them to the vendor to be put back into circulation. The practice of offering milagros is still common today, and Hispanic churches across the Southwest are filled with them. Believers attach them to every imaginable surface on the inside of the church: walls, shrines, crosses, altars, the clothing of saints.

The milagro traces its roots to the ancient past. Since prehistoric times people have made votive offerings to deities in the shape of small people, body parts, animals, and objects, in hopes that the diety will intervene on their behalf. Interestingly, Native Americans shared a similar practice of crafting amulets and votive offerings, and proffering them in hopes of protection or divine favor. Centuries before Christ, people inhabiting what is now Spain used amulets very similar to the ones still made today. After Christianity took root, the custom was reappropriated for Christian use. It became common throughout Spanish colonial Mexico, and the practice was transported to the new Hispanic communities in the Southwest.

Milagros are crafted of many materials, from tin to gold, silver, iron, pewter, wood, wax, or any other material. Usually they are stamped from a mold, and the same designs can be found repeatedly. Today, milagros are often incorporated into contemporary jewelry designs, and they are sometimes given as gifts or to convey meaning; for example, you might give a heart to someone who is undergoing a heart operation.

Another type of traditional votive offering is the retablo ex-voto. These scenes, usually painted on tin panels or even animal hides, portray images of miracles or of the supplicant praying for a miracle. In a band along the bottom, text explains what is happening in the scene or offers a personalized prayer. Antique examples are highly collectible and can command high prices at folk art auctions and galleries specializing in Hispanic craft.

Relicarios, or lockets worn on chains, represent a lesser-known but still important craft tradition. In the Old World, reliquaries of the Middle Ages contained a piece of a saint's bone or other relic in a small boxlike contraption. In the New World, Spanish and Portuguese colonists wore relicarios—minus the relic—as a locket fashioned with images of saints; these provided comfort and protection against the dangers of life on the frontier. Today, these are rare but most of the good regional museums have them in their collections, and you may find them in antique stores or flea markets if you're lucky.

With the arrival of mass-produced commercial goods at the end of the 1800s, many innovative craftspeople began combining modern media with these old-fashioned religious works. Today, look for wonderfully creative devotional works incorporating photographs, lithographs, magazine clips, and found objects.

THE REAL DEAL

Milagros are a real steal. You can buy them for less than a dollar at some of the Hispanic craft dealers in the Southwest. Antique, custom, or rare examples command higher prices.

CREAM OF THE CROP

La Hormiga Blanca in Tucson (page 115) offers big baskets full of milagros, as well as crosses and other objects encrusted with them.

SAVVY SHOPPER

Once you familiarize yourself with common themes of milagros, it's fun to rummage through piles of them in search of unusual and even bizarre examples.

STRAW CRAFTS

O ne of the hallmarks of Hispanic New Mexican craftspeople throughout history has been their ingenuity in crafting beautiful and precious-seeming objects out of very simple materials. There could be no better example than the myriad crafts created and decorated with dried straw.

Straw design has been practiced since the early 1700s by both Hispanic and Native American populations. Straw was a cheap alternative to precious metals such as silver or gold, which were not readily available as natural resources, and were expensive and dangerous to transport from Mexico. Local artisans were challenged to use their ingenuity to create "luxury" products from very modest materials.

There are two main techniques of Hispanic straw crafts. Straw appliqué or inlay refers to dried straw that is glued to a wooden object—usually a cross but sometimes a chest, box, or retablo, usually painted black for a contrasting effect. The process begins by carving out shallow indentations from the object, into which the dried straw is carefully glued into elaborate patterns.

Encrusted straw refers to dried straw that is applied decoratively to the flat surfaces of crosses or retablos, then covered with varnish to preserve the piece and impart a glossy finish. Sometimes other plants, such as corn or wheat, are incorporated into this painstaking craft.

The techniques are closely related to European marquetry, in which thin layers of different-colored woods, ivory, tortoiseshell, mother-of-pearl, and other materials are applied to create decorative patterns on furniture and wooden objects. There is very little written documentation and few surviving examples of the earliest straw crafts, but colonial New Mexican craftspeople probably had some knowledge of marquetry due to their contact with Spanish and Portuguese settlers.

Straw work seems to have declined in the 1800s, but the passion for it was revived in the 1920s, thanks to a handful of craftspeople. Today few historical examples survive, but contemporary artisans carry on the tradition. The Santa Fe Spanish Market offers one of the few opportunities to appreciate a wide range of this extraordinarily beautiful and ephemeral work.

THE REAL DEAL

Crosses are the most common vehicle for straw decoration, often with an incredibly intricate series of geometric or vegetal designs. Other historically authentic objects decorated with straw appliqué include boxes, chests, and panels.

CREAM OF THE CROP

Saints & Martyrs in Albuquerque (page 140) or Santa Fe's annual Spanish Market (page 189) are among a limited number of places to find straw crafts.

TEXTILES

oday it is hard to imagine thousands of sheep herds dotting the southwestern landscape, but preindustrial Hispanic society relied on farming and herding *churro* sheep as the basis of its economy. Given the abundant supply of wool, it's no surprise that weaving became one of the most prolific crafts practiced in the pre-industrial Hispanic Southwest.

Largely a woman's art, colonial weaving included rugs, bedding, clothing, blankets, church decorations, and many other utilitarian works. By the early nineteenth century many New Mexican textiles were exported south to Mexico and farther afield. In turn, Mexican weavers traveled north to share their knowledge with settlers in the colony.

Simple weaving looms—usually traditional four-harness, counterbalanced floor looms—were constructed out of rough-hewn logs and later milled lumber with metal fittings. These contraptions have changed little since Spanish colonists brought them to the New World. Weavers created four basic types of fabrics from these looms: a heavy material used for grain sacks, wagon covers, and packing called *sayal*; a finer-weave white wool used for clothing and bedding called *sabanilla*; *bayeta*, used for clothing; and *jerga*, used for lesser-quality clothes and rugs. Weavers used natural vegetable and mineral dyes initially; they switched to commercially available dyes, which provided a larger range of colors, after the mid-nineteenth century.

Numerous and complex weaving styles developed over the years. "Rio Grande blankets" is now a general term that refers to the entire weaving tradition of Hispanic New Mexico. However, these rugs often are highly localized traditions, and each town boasts its own distinctive pattern and color combinations. Important centers include Chimayó, an old Hispanic settlement that has evolved as a weaving center over more than three hundred years.

Embroidery also emerged as an important craft in the Hispanic Southwest. The *colcha* stitch became one of the most characteristic techniques in the Hispanic textile tradition. This time-consuming stitch is a form of embroidery in which the embroiderer makes a long, straight stitch in the fabric, then crosses it in the middle at a right or diagonal angle, anchoring the long stitch into the fabric.

The colcha stitch seems to have emerged in the early 1700s, but it is uncertain where it originated. Some historians have pointed to similarities between the colcha stitch and stitches used in Oriental silks, Turkish textiles, and East Indian chintz. It seems more likely that Spanish and Mexican examples served as prototypes, although many of those derived forms from examples they imported into Spain from the East over the course of the 1600s and 1700s. Today, the colcha stitch flourishes on silks, wall hangings, and clothing, a testament to the strong and enduring textile industry in the Hispanic Southwest.

═══ CHEAT SHEET: HISPANIC WEAVINGS ═══

Here are some of the more common traditional Hispanic weaving styles that you can still find across the Southwest:

• **Chimayó**: two stripes and symmetrical, central geometric designs
• **Jerga**: coarse, loosely woven, often with simple black-and-white or brown-and-white checkered patterns
• **Moki**: characterized by alternating horizontal bands of color
• **Saltillo**: fine, expensive tapestries developed in Mexico, and popular in the early to mid-1800s, usually with a border and central diamond pattern
• **Tree of Life**: tree with birds on the limbs, also seen in Navajo weavings
• **Vallero**: weavings with a border and distinctive eight-pointed-star pattern, popular in the late 1800s

CREAM OF THE CROP

The Trujillo family at Centinela Traditional Arts in Chimayó (page 145) has been practicing the craft for several generations and is one of the premier families of traditional weaving in the country.

SAVVY SHOPPER

Hispanic weavings can command high prices. Small contemporary weavings start at a few hundred dollars; expect to pay at least $1,000 for a rug-size piece. Fine antique pieces can draw five figures.

TINWARE AND METALWORK

Spanish colonists hoped to find significant deposits of silver and gold as they moved north along the Rio Grande. In fact, historical documents show that silversmiths ready to put their skills to work figured among the early entourages. However, the limited sources of silver and gold they found could not be mined on a large scale until the arrival of new technology, toward the end of the nineteenth century. In the meantime, settlers used silver pieces they brought from Mexico, mostly utilitarian household utensils such as candlestick holders and tableware.

Once tin arrived in great quantities along with the Anglo-Americans in the nineteenth century, this new material prompted the excellent Hispanic metalsmiths to put their skills to work. Known as "poor man's silver," tin has enjoyed a fertile history among Hispanic craftspeople of the Southwest. While the majority of Hispanic crafts suffered because of the influx of commercial products in the nineteenth century, tin crafts actually flourished as a result. The new availability of British tinplate and the arrival of Anglo tinsmiths influenced the craft. Artisans began collecting tin cans, recycling them into utilitarian and decorative objects ranging from crosses, boxes, sconces for candles, frames, and other objects.

Most tinware was crafted for religious purposes—frames for religious prints, devotional crosses, and church ornaments. By the late 1800s traditional painted retablos fell out of favor in some places; instead, religious prints in decorative tin frames were preferred. Today you can find an appealing array of decorative tin crafts, from candle sconces punched with small holes that flicker with light to unique Christmas ornaments, framed mirrors, centerpieces, and other items.

CREAM OF THE CROP

At the Tinsmith in Old Town San Diego (page 125) you can watch artisans craft authentic tin frames, sconces, ornaments, and other goods on the premises.

SAVVY SHOPPER

Tinware is available at relatively reasonable prices. For under $50 you can choose from a wide array of options, from ornaments to frames.

WROUGHT IRON

T
he American Southwest is not rich in iron ore, but the blacksmith's craft was so critical in preindustrial society that wrought iron craft flourished in early New Mexico nonetheless. Metalsmiths were among the early contingents of colonists who migrated north along the Rio Grande in the 1500s. They brought with them small iron implements, tools, hardware, and other trinkets to trade with the Pueblo Indians, who placed a high value on these objects.

Once Hispanic communities were established, the settlers relied mostly on iron in the form of bars and sheets imported from Spain. In part, the reliance on imported iron was imposed by the Spanish crown, which wanted to protect Spain's own iron industry. Because of the scant quantities of available iron, metalsmiths adapted their work. Compared with larger and more elaborate examples produced by their Mexican neighbors, these colonists crafted smaller and more modest implements, furniture, and hardware.

Hispanic metalsmiths applied their distinctive and familiar vocabulary of forms to craft objects of restrained, rustic beauty. They focused on objects of devotion—crosses and church ornamentation—as well as large-scale architectural works such as gates for churches, and grand entrances to homes and to communities walled with adobe.

The metalsmith's craft is ancient, and its techniques have changed little over time. Even today, traditional metalsmiths rely on the same tools used for thousands of years—a furnace or forge, an anvil to use as a base for shaping iron works, and a variety of hammers and chisels to cut, flatten, or fashion a particular form. No longer relied upon for the basic tools of living, metalsmiths now ply their trade by making decorative and custom work.

Hispanic metalsmiths passed on their skills not only to their children but also to Native Americans. As part of the Spanish king's colonial strategy, craftspeople were instructed to teach Native Americans their trades, and by the seventeenth century metalsmith shops could be found within Native American communities across New Mexico.

THE REAL DEAL

At the Spanish Market in Santa Fe (page 189), you'll enjoy direct access to Hispanic metalsmiths who do not run a retail space of their own and whose work you might not find elsewhere.

SAVVY SHOPPER

Wrought iron crafts are a relatively good value, especially when you consider the ease with which you can commission a custom piece such as a gate or furniture hardware. Antique hinges, drawer pulls, and other small forged works can also be picked up cheaply from antiques dealers and markets across the Southwest.

NATIVE AMERICAN CRAFTS

Craftsmanship is one of the most enduring indigenous historical traditions of the Americas. Humans have inhabited the Southwest for millennia. Many trades were already highly developed centuries ago, as evidenced in the startlingly rich finds of pottery and other handmade wares in archeological sites across the Southwest. Many of these works are preserved to a degree that would not be possible elsewhere in the country, thanks to a relatively arid climate that minimizes the damaging effects created by moisture in the soil and humidity in the air.

For some two thousand years the Anasazi people occupied the area now known as Four Corners, so named because it forms right angles where Colorado, New Mexico, Arizona, and Utah meet. The Anasazi are thought to be the ancestors of the modern Native Americans of New Mexico and Arizona. The Anasazi seem to have migrated southward in the 1300s, but they left thousands of ruins behind, suggesting a culture of sophistication in both architecture and crafts, especially pottery. Contemporary Pueblo people carry on the legacy of the Anasazi in their community-based lifestyle and craft traditions. The Hopi, a separate people, established villages atop mesas in Arizona some seven hundred years ago. The agriculturally based Navajo and Apache arrived in the 1400s, continuing the tradition of creating cliff dwellings, as well as settling pueblos as the center of community life.

When Spanish explorers and missionaries entered the Southwest in the mid-1500s, the clash of the two worlds—Native American and Hispanic—resulted in a fascinating exchange of manual trades that would affect the development of crafts of both cultures over the next centuries. Some historians believe that Hispanic craftspeople learned to carve santos from the roots of cottonwood trees, in a similar way that the Hopi crafted their katsinas. Spanish missionaries brought Roman Catholicism to the pueblos, along with its related trades—church building, saint making, iron forging. Native Americans learned metalsmithing techniques from the Spanish, and the influence pushed their own craft traditions in new directions, especially in jewelry. Santa Fe was settled around 1610, and the city became a major trading center between Native American and Hispanic populations. Exchanges were not always peaceful; the indigenous populations resisted the Spanish colonists on many different occasions, notably during the 1680 pueblo revolt that drove the

Spanish back south to El Paso. Nonetheless, cultural exchanges continued to influence the artisanal traditions of both cultures.

By the time New Mexico was ceded to the United States at the end of the Mexican-American War in 1848, tourism had already begun to develop in the Southwest. Visitors were eager to buy and bring home the unique pottery, jewelry, and other goods of the Native Americans. The Smithsonian and other East Coast museums mounted expeditions to collect pieces from what many surmised would soon be an extinct population. By the 1890s, amateur archeologists scoured the countryside for pottery with picks in hand, and traders sold the pieces by mail order until the U.S. government passed a law forbidding excavation on federal lands in 1906.

The demand for indigenous crafts among Anglo collectors and tourists spawned a new economy for Native American artisans that would change the face of Indian craftsmanship. Instead of creating vessels exclusively for domestic or ceremonial use, potters began creating wares specifically for the tourist market, using patterns and colors popular with the Anglo consumer. Zuni carvers reserved special fetishes for their own ceremonial use, and created other ones for tourists. They developed new, nontraditional subject matter they felt would appeal to this new market hungry for Native American crafts. This evolution has continued to the present day.

Anglo culture created another important institution that influenced Native American crafts: the trading post and "Indian pawn." The curious tradition of Indian pawn began with the trading posts that set up shop across the Southwest in the nineteenth century. The pawn system was an economic arrangement in which the trader acted like a bank to Native Americans. By the 1870s traders accepted Indian crafts—usually jewelry, but also other pieces with intrinsic value such as rugs—in trade for things they needed, including groceries or other provisions. When they had some cash, most owners would buy back their pawned jewelry. This system is still active today.

Is It Authentic?

There are strict rules about crafting and selling Native American wares that are sold as "authentic." You can file a complaint to the Indian Arts and Crafts Board of the U.S. Department of the Interior if you believe an individual or business is violating the Indian Arts and Crafts Act, which protects the intellectual and creative rights of Native American craftspeople. Always ask for a written guarantee of authenticity from the dealer; if he or she refuses, move on.

In spite of the many outside cultural influences that have touched the Southwest's indigenous populations over the past five hundred years, today's Pueblo Indians retain a surprisingly precolonial and preindustrial way of life. The basic fabric of community life, as well as many of its centuries-old craft traditions, remains much as it was before the Spanish set foot on native lands.

The longevity of the artisanal traditions, as well as the limited availability of these objects (there aren't as many Native Americans as there used to be), no doubt has influenced the prices of Native American crafts, among the most highly valued in our culture. Today's collector's market for Native American crafts is stronger than ever before, and prices can be steep, especially for highly valued items such as Navajo rugs and quality pueblo pottery.

Revival of interest in Native American crafts in the 1960s and 1970s, along with Native Americans' renewed interest in their own cultural heritage and collective identity, has done the most to promote and preserve these craft traditions. Numerous organizations are in the business of protecting and promoting authentic Native American craftsmanship. Among the most important are the Indian Arts and Crafts Association (IACA), the Indian Arts and Crafts Board of the U.S. Department of the Interior, and the Council for Indigenous Arts and Culture.

===== INDIAN PAWN: A LIVING TRADITION =====

Today, the tradition of Indian pawn—in which a trader accepts Native American jewelry or other crafts in exchange for provisions—lives on. According to many traders, the vast majority of pawned pieces are bought back by the original owners at a later date. After a certain period of time, unclaimed items are considered "dead pawn" and may be put up for sale. Across the Southwest, trading post "pawn rooms" have some of the most interesting collections of objects to browse—treasure troves of squash blossom necklaces, leather saddles, concha belts, and sometimes thousands of other items old and new.

BASKETS

C ommon to all Native Americans of the Southwest, basket weaving is a long-standing and important craft tradition. For many centuries, southwestern Native Americans have created and used baskets for utilitarian purposes like gathering, preparing, and storing food. Certain vessels also serve a ceremonial use. Mostly a woman's art, basketry has passed down through the generations from grandmothers to mothers and daughters. Today, some men are involved in crafting baskets as well.

Using materials as varied as cottonwood, willow, rabbit brush, or reeds, grasses, and sticks, today's artisans carry on a long tradition of creating baskets using techniques including coiling and braiding. The artisan must have in mind the design he or she wants to create before starting. Geometrical and organic decoration are the most common, along with zigzags, leaf patterns, diamonds, step patterns, and stripes. Colors were originally derived from plant dyes the Native Americans knew about from dyeing textiles and other objects; today, some artisans continue to adhere to the traditional dyes. Beads, feathers, and other objects sometimes are incorporated into the weave.

Plaiting is the simplest technique basket weavers use, weaving each strand over and under to create a checkerboard-like effect. Twining is a technique similar to textile weaving, as it involves weaving a more flexible strand through a web of stronger ones. Finally, coiling is the most common technique used today. In this technique, the basket maker begins with a single stick or rod, and coils the material around it, then coils the stick into a circle spiraling out from the center. Many of the most beautiful Native American coiled baskets are flat or nearly flat, while other popular forms include small wastebasket-like vessels with lids. The Apache are known for their cone-shaped burden baskets, worn on the back by women during their daily search for food among the plants and crops near their villages.

The Hopi, especially artisans in the villages of the Second and Third Mesas, are particularly renowned for their rich tradition of coiled basket making. Baskets play an important role in ceremonial and traditional Hopi life. When a couple is engaged, the bride and her mother present a coiled, flattened basket to the groom's mother, piled high with blue-corn piki bread. The basket is a treasured possession and kept throughout the couple's lives. Traditional colored designs include katsinas, eagles, lightning, and other motifs.

Good values can be had on the baskets made by the Tohono O'odham people, located on a remote reservation southwest of Tucson. The hallmark of this weaving style is using the natural colors of the plants and reeds in decorative patterns. Unusual shapes such as human figures and animals add a whimsical element to their weaving.

Before the end of the nineteenth century, collectors had little interest in Native American baskets. However, around that time the idea circulated among Anglo collectors that the Native American populations might not survive over the long term. Suddenly, consumers began amassing collections of baskets and as many other crafts as they could acquire. This new interest in the craft spawned the best of Native American creativity, as artisans experimented with new forms and materials to respond to this new audience hungry for their work. By the early twentieth century, Native American basketry was being produced primarily in the service of the tourist and collectors' markets, and much less for local use. Today, however, there also is renewed interest in these beautiful and delicate works within Native American communities themselves.

THE REAL DEAL

A high-quality basket is distinguished by the tightness and fineness of the weave (measured in stitches per inch), as well as a symmetrical shape. Antique baskets often fetch higher prices than contemporary ones, depending on their condition, size, and origin. Watch out for baskets made in Pakistan, which look surprisingly similar to Native American baskets and appear in shops throughout the Southwest. If it costs less than $100, chances are it was not made on the pueblo.

CREAM OF THE CROP

The Hubbell Trading Post in Ganado (page 100) carries a nice selection of Native American coiled baskets at fair prices.

SAVVY SHOPPER

Prices for authentic Native American baskets can be steep. On the Hopi mesas, expect to pay upward of $1,000 or more for a quality coiled basket.

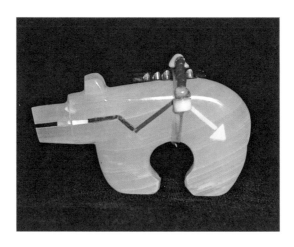

FETISHES

Though many Native American groups make fetishes, the Zuni have distinguished themselves in their carving skill and the sheer quantity and variety of their fetishes.

Fetishes are animal-shaped carvings that the Zuni people believe to possess the spirit of a being with powers to heal and help their owners. The Zuni have been carving these diminutive creatures for at least a millennium, usually from bone, marble, jet, serpentine, turquoise, wood, or stone. The use of fetishes among the Zuni and other Native American peoples seems to have been one way of gaining control over erratic forces of nature.

According to Zuni legend, a pair of Warrior Twins in the remote past slew predator animals with their bows and arrows, turning them to stone. Traditionally, a series of these animal archetypes is represented in Zuni fetishes, each with its own symbology. Zuni fetishes are often festooned with feathers, arrowheads, or inlaid turquoise and other gems—offerings to make them more effective. Some fetishes also have "heartlines" carved from the mouth across the body. There are several interpretations of this, which include giving the fetish healing power or representing lightning.

With the advent of electrical carving tools, new subjects have been invented; for example, deer and elk were not traditionally sculpted in the past because of the difficulty of carving long skinny legs and antlers using the old tools. Today they are more common.

Sacred fetishes—those that have been blessed by a Zuni holy man—are never sold but may be offered as a gift, often to children. Owners carry them in their pocket, or keep them inside a pot or other special place at home. Most fetishes, however, are made to be sold to visitors or outsiders. Today there are some three hundred fetish carvers in the Zuni Pueblo of western New Mexico, who sell their wares to visitors and distribute them to dealers across the Southwest to the delight of collectors of these wondrous little objects.

THE REAL DEAL

Few authentic Zuni fetishes are signed, although signed pieces are becoming more prevalent. Counterfeit fetishes are mass-produced in Asia, so always buy from a reputable dealer.

CREAM OF THE CROP

The Zuni Pueblo (page 127) can create a custom fetish just for you.

SAVVY SHOPPER

Zuni fetishes generally run $70 to several hundred dollars, depending on the artist and the subject. While each person may interpret the meaning of his or her fetish differently, most have a traditional association. Here are some of the more common beasts you'll encounter:

- **badger**: represents the south
- **bear**: the most humanlike of animals, represents the west
- **bobcat**: predator of the south
- **coyote**: predator of the west
- **eagle**: associated with the zenith or sky
- **mole**: represents the nadir or netherworld
- **mountain lion**: represents the north; one of the oldest carved beasts
- **wolf**: associated with the east

KATSINA (OR KACHINA) DOLLS

Small carved wooden figures, known as katsina or kachina dolls (katsinam in the plural), are common to the Pueblo peoples, especially the Hopi. Katsinam represent supernatural beings with the power to bring a bountiful harvest, good health, prosperity, and other positive things to their owners and to the entire tribe. They represent beings from animals to humans—or sometimes part animal, part human—in a strict hierarchy. Traditionally katsinam are given as gifts to infant boys and to girls of all ages, probably as a way to help them learn the stories and characters in the katsina hierarchy and to bestow the benefits associated with a particular katsina.

Katsinam play an important role in the ceremonial life of the Hopi, who look to them for good health, copious crops, and other good fortune. From winter solstice through the spring season, Hopi men dance in ceremonies elaborately dressed as life-size katsinam, summoned by the tribe for good fortune. The first katsina in the Hopi calendar appears at winter solstice, and other important ceremonial events take place in February (the Powamuya or Bean Dance) and July (the Niman or Home Dance). Many of the rituals take place in the kiva, a partially underground ceremonial space often entered by ladder through the ceiling. After this cycle of ritual, the legends say that the katsinam return to their home in the San Francisco peaks.

According to Hopi legend, the katsinam themselves make the carvings. Traditionally representations of these benevolent spirits were roughly carved from *paako*, the roots of cottonwood trees; they were then sanded with stone and painted with plant pigments. They did not have a base to stand on and were often hung on the wall. Over time, the designs got more elaborate and sophisticated, and the creatures took on more realistic characteristics. In the twentieth century, artisans began to portray katsina dolls in more active poses—dancing, shooting arrows, and doing other dramatic activities. Katsinam are sometimes adorned with everything from a simple feather to elaborate costumes of cloth, fur, and beadwork. Since the 1970s, however, there has been an increasing trend to return to the simpler, more traditional forms and techniques of the preindustrial age.

Some of today's katsina carvers, mostly men, use a variety of knives and sandpaper to carve the pine or cottonwood roots (the same material coveted by Hispanic santeros, or makers of santos; see page 36). Some take advantage of modern electric carving tools to create intricate detail. Today, many artisans use commercially available paints, though a few insist on traditional plant dyes.

As early as the mid-nineteenth century Anglo collectors showed an interest in collecting katsina dolls. Today they are very popular collector's items and many Hopi artisans make a living solely by creating these traditional carvings.

Katsina carvings are also made by other Native American groups, including the Navajo and the Zuni, but the Hopi are the most renowned for this craft. The Hopi First Mesa is a center of katsina production, and you can watch these beguiling figures being made when craftsmen open their homes to visitors.

CHEAT SHEET: HOPI KATSINAM

There are some 250 katsinam traditional to the Hopi, though many more have been invented in recent years. Here is a list of some of the most common traditional examples you'll see:
- **badger**: a healer associated with medicinal plants
- **bear**: thought to have healing powers, usually with a bear print on his face
- **corn**: important personifications celebrated in connection with planting and harvest
- **grandmother**: the matriarch of katsinam, popular as a gift for girls
- **owl**: one of many bird katsinam, portrayed as a warrior
- **solstice**: opens the katsina season at winter solstice

THE REAL DEAL

There is a vigorous trade in mass-produced katsina dolls made in factories or at least by non-Hopi carvers. Whenever possible, buy directly from the artisan or a reputable dealer of Hopi art.

CREAM OF THE CROP

Keams Canyon's McGee's Indian Art (page 101) carries some nice but expensive realistic katsinam. The Hubbell Trading Post in Ganado (page 100) carries more affordable and more traditional, simpler examples. Or, visit First or Second Mesa and buy directly from a carver working in his home.

SAVVY SHOPPER

Prices for authentic Hopi katsinam are steep. Many people get hooked on collecting these wonderful spirit-creatures, however, and will gladly pay the common asking price of $1,000 to $2,500 each.

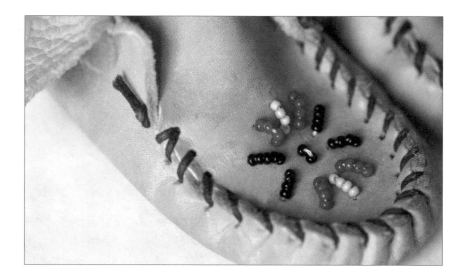

JEWELRY AND BEADWORK

N ative Americans have valued certain stones and shells for many centuries, incorporating them into beautiful and distinctive jewelry designs that have evolved in many directions over time. In addition to turquoise, and often paired with this gem, coral, pearls, and spiny oyster shell were actively traded with tribes of the West Coast.

Turquoise occupies a special place in southwestern jewelry. Native American artisans have been using the blue stone for more than two thousand years. Native Americans mined the sky-colored stone, once plentiful and now nearly depleted, by digging deep into the ground using antlers and other hand-fashioned tools. The Turquoise Trail between Albuquerque and Santa Fe held many ancient but now defunct turquoise mines, including Cerrillos and Madrid.

There are many legends and popular beliefs about turquoise. For many, turquoise means power; the Zuni often attached a small piece of the stone to their fetish figures to enhance their potency. According to one Hopi legend, turquoise was the excrement of lizards, a highly revered animal. Navajo myths say that when the wind is blowing, it is searching for turquoise, and that wearing turquoise brings good luck and protection from illness. Many Native American tribes associated turquoise with bringing rain. It is no surprise that trading turquoise has been a bustling industry for many centuries.

Jewelry dealers usually refer to the stones in their jewelry by the name of the mine from which they originated. Some of the more commonly found stones in the Southwest come from Bisbee, Sleeping Beauty, Orvil Jack, Cerrillos, and Kingman. Today, the Sleeping Beauty Mine in Miami, Arizona, is the only natural source of turquoise in that state. As a result, many artisans must resort to private stashes of turquoise hawked by stone dealers or using stones from older jewelry pieces. More often, they use natural or stabilized turquoise imported from mines in China or other countries.

This distinctive stone is created when water seeps through a porous rock and reacts with aluminum, copper, and iron in a way that is still not precisely understood. The range of colors is stunning, from bright to dark and light blue to green and yellow, and even white. Part of the "host rock" or other minerals can create fissures and interesting patterns in the turquoise referred to as a matrix.

At first Native Americans fashioned beads of the stone, or incorporated them into fetishes and ceremonial objects. When the Spanish introduced silversmithing to the pueblos, Native American artisans married the silver and turquoise to create stunning creations that persist to the present day. To get silver originally, they melted down Mexican pesos, valued for their high silver content, that they acquired through trade. By the mid-twentieth century, the majority of Native American jewelry craftspeople used sterling silver, a mixture of soft, pure silver, and copper, which hardens it. Silver jewelry predominates throughout the Southwest. Most of it is sterling silver, and it is sometimes, but not always, stamped with the words "sterling" or ".925" on the back. Often the artist's hallmark is also stamped into the piece. The silver sheets can be hammered, or melted down and poured into a mold to create the desired shape, giving the artisan maximum leverage to exercise his or her creativity.

THE REAL DEAL
Jewelry artisans in Santo Domingo Pueblo still craft the ancient form of *heishi*, beads shaped like hockey pucks that are closely stacked and threaded on multistrand necklaces.

CREAM OF THE CROP
The stores of Navajo Arts & Crafts Enterprise (pages 99, 101, and 119) are a good place to pick up small beaded objects.

The Hopi have excelled at silversmithing since the 1930s, when they began using an overlay process that allowed them to create designs with raised silver against a darker background. Today, they still craft special and easily recognizable silver inlay and overlay works, often stamped with the artist's hallmark. Hopi artisans on Second Mesa have made a name for themselves in silver overlay jewelry. The Zuni are also renowned for jewelry of stone, often incorporating small fetishes into bracelets and necklaces. Traditionally the Navajo create very symmetrical silver pieces, often with a central design and stone.

As you browse through stores across the Southwest, you will recognize many traditional jewelry designs. One of the most characteristic is the squash blossom necklace. The centerpiece of the necklace is a crescent—a downward-facing horseshoe called a *naja*—often encrusted with turquoise, silver beads, or both, with beaded "squash blossoms" of silver along the necklace strands. The squash blossom is part of a long mythology of the Navajo, but the necklace as we know it wasn't codified until the end of the 1800s. Jewelry historians believe that the naja developed from small iron horseshoes that ornamented the horse bridles of the Spanish conquistadors and were traded with the Native Americans, who wore them around their necks. Over time many have ascribed different meanings to the squash blossom necklaces, from agricultural fruitfulness to a woman's fertility, but there is no one interpretation.

In addition to jewelry, the related craft of beadwork is also an important tradition for many Native Americans of the Southwest. The earliest beads were crafted of turquoise and other stones, seeds, nuts, animal teeth or claws, and bones. Beads made of seashells were used throughout the pueblos and particularly prized in the landlocked regions. The beads were a valuable trade item with tribes from the West Coast, as the shells symbolized the life-giving force of water. The incredible variety of ancient beads discovered all over the United States is a testament to the vast trade routes already well developed centuries ago.

Beads were of course strung together for necklaces and bracelets, but eventually beadwork decorated every imaginable surface, from clothing to shoes, jewelry, textiles, pouches, and baskets. Although leather formed a popular base for working bead designs, you'll find exquisite beadwork on unlikely objects such as dried gourds, which are particularly beautiful.

The Spanish recognized the value of beads to the locals, and records from the sixteenth century show that the early Spanish colonists came equipped with glass beads to trade with the natives. Glass beads continued to be popular in later centuries, and are still among the most common beads used by today's beadwork artisans, many of whom are women.

=== CHEAT SHEET: GRADING TURQUOISE ===

By law, there are five grades of turquoise on the market today:

• **natural**: hard, perfect stones that are mined, polished, and set. Natural turquoise represents a minuscule percentage of the stones on today's market; in fact, it is rarer than diamonds. The harder the stone, the more valuable it is.

• **stabilized**: soft or chalky turquoise that has been stabilized with clear epoxy to harden it, a technique developed in the 1960s. Most of the turquoise in reputable shops has undergone this process.

• **treated**: stabilized turquoise that includes colored epoxy resin to affect the color of the stone. Ancient artisans sometimes added oils or wax to turquoise.

• **reconstituted**: low-quality turquoise that has been ground into powder, then compressed into blocks

• **imitation**: plastic, glass, or composite materials, often imported and set into authentic-looking silver jewelry

It is often difficult without laboratory analysis to tell what kind of treatment a stone has undergone. A reputable dealer will provide you with a description of your stones in writing, indicating which mine they came from and the grade.

THE REAL DEAL

The following are some of the main techniques used in Native American jewelry:

• **appliqué**: decorative designs soldered onto a piece, popular with Navajo silversmiths

• **castwork**: molten silver poured into a casting of sand or stone to create a design

• **clusterwork**: extremely intricate clusters achieved with silver and tiny stones, common in Zuni jewelry

• **hammering and stamp work**: stamping patterns into hot and soft metal, often used to achieve repetitive patterns as in concha belts

• **"liquid silver"**: a tedious process of stringing minuscule rod-shaped silver beads on a thin cord

• **overlay**: two pieces soldered together, with a cutout design in the top revealing a contrasting metal underneath

• **repoussé**: a technique of stamping from the back of the piece so that from the front the decorative parts appear raised

Just like buying diamonds and other precious stones, the best way to ensure the quality and authenticity of your piece is to buy from a reputable dealer. You should also ask the dealer to write on your receipt where the piece was made, what kind and grade of stone is used, the name of the artist, if known, and any other relevant information.

SAVVY SHOPPER

Check out the Indian pawn rooms of trading posts and jewelry shops across the Southwest for unique antique pieces. Among the antique pieces you may even find a natural, untreated stone from a Southwest mine, quite a rarity today.

POTTERY

L iterally volumes have been penned about pueblo pottery, and it is arguably the richest and most complex craft tradition of the Southwest's Native Americans. This section, though longer than many others in this book, only scratches the surface of this dynamic tradition.

Decorated pottery originated centuries ago among the native peoples of Arizona and New Mexico. For more than two millennia, pots have held food and water, and have played an important role in ceremonies. Decorated vessels, most often created by women, were also traded among tribes. Based on the archeological evidence of ancient pots across the Southwest, some of today's pots owe their stylistic heritage to the ancient forebears of today's modern Native tribes—the Anasazi, the Hohokam, and the Mogollon.

While there is some variation in technique, all Native American pots begin with the gathering of local clay, which is sorted, sifted, and soaked. Other materials such as sand, rock, horsehair, or shards of other pots are incorporated into the mix. This laborious preparation also includes soaking the dried clay in a water bath for several days, then straining it across a metal screen to make it the perfect consistency for working by hand.

THE REAL DEAL

Through the 1960s, few Native American potters signed their works, but after the fame achieved by Maria Martinez and a few others, the trend gained in popularity. Today, it is increasingly common for potters to sign their works, and you can expect to pay more for signed pieces. However, just because a pot is unsigned does not mean you shouldn't buy it. Indeed, many of the best values in Native American pottery today are in unsigned works.

SAVVY SHOPPER

Signed pots by Maria Martinez fetch five-figure sums at auction today. Over the last three decades, many other individuals and families have made names for themselves and their pottery is highly coveted by collectors. Unsigned pots or those signed by little-known potters in typical traditional styles can be had for a few hundred to a few thousand dollars.

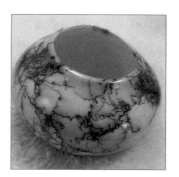

When the clay is ready, the potter may build the vessel freehand, or place it in a basket or shallow hole in the ground to help form it. She then winds a rope of clay into the shape, then presses the clay with her hands or a knifelike instrument to smooth its surface. After the pot hardens, the potter sands it with a smooth stone, and may incise a design, or color or paint it using slip created with dyes from local plants, including yucca and beeweed. The piece is usually dried in the sun before firing.

THE REAL DEAL
Factors that affect a pot's value include size, uniformity, figural decoration, presence or lack of cracks or lumps, and whether or not the potter is well known.

CREAM OF THE CROP
Andrea Fisher Fine Pottery in Santa Fe (page 154) is one of the region's most well-respected dealers of quality pueblo pottery.

SAVVY SHOPPER
Some dealers will accept a "trade in" of your old pots and other Native American wares.

Firing takes place either over an open fire or in an earthenware kiln. Sheep or cow dung is used for fuel, placed around the pots, and ignited. Generally pottery fired on an open fire commands higher prices, since it represents the older tradition.

Each pueblo boasts traditional and customary styles that are easily distinguished from one another. Today, more than two dozen distinctive styles can be discerned. There is a whole typology of vessels from ceremonial bowls to bean pots, fetish jars, and melon jars. There are many more types and regional styles, each of which has warranted at least one book-length treatment. However, that does not mean that every artisan in a single pueblo creates the same style, and there is a wide range of individuality. The most well-recognized styles are the black-on-black ware popularized by Maria Martinez of San Ildefonso Pueblo over the course of the twentieth century; the geometrically decorated black-and-white pots of Acoma; and the mottled pots of Picuris. For ease, I have organized the major pottery styles into rough cultural groups on the following pages.

ACOMA, SANTO DOMINGO, COCHITÍ, ZIA, SANTA ANA, AND JEMEZ PUEBLOS

The Keres-speaking peoples occupy pueblos located west and southwest of Santa Fe. They are recognized for pots covered in opaque cream-colored slip, a watery clay that coats the surface and makes it smooth, and that are then decorated with patterns or figures in black and red.

Potters in Acoma and Santo Domingo Pueblos boast the most well-known works of this group. As the oldest continuously inhabited settlement in North America, Acoma Pueblo occupies a high mesa with a beautiful church in its ancient center, Sky City. Its artisans are known for their distinctive black-and-white designs, often in an allover geometric pattern. The signature of the pueblo is the large, round vessel called an *olla*. The local slatelike clay, when fired, turns bright white, providing a contrast to the black geometric decoration.

Santo Domingo is another major tradition that distinguishes itself with large geometric designs of red, black, and cream. Larger-scale pots recall ancient Greek pottery in their size, elegant shapes, and geometric bands of decoration of flowers and leaves. Pots that are created for sale usually do not depict animals or human figures; these are reserved for ceremonial use.

The Cochití and other Keres-speaking peoples are known for crafting figurines of animals and people. The black-on-cream palette characterizes the decoration of these wares, and human faces and costumes have lots of character. In the 1960s, Helen Cordero invented "storytellers," a female figure surrounded by children listening intently to her stories. Now Cochití Pueblo has refocused its ceramic production on storyteller figurines and is turning them out mostly for the tourist trade and collectors.

At Zia, potters temper the clay with basalt to create an exceptionally hard pot. Their hallmark is the fast Zia bird, a sacred animal that brings prayers to the deities. Other motifs include spiderwebs, feathers, and clouds.

The pottery traditions of Santa Ana and Jemez have been nearly lost, but because of the revived interest in traditional crafts, native artisans are experimenting with new materials and styles to appeal to today's thriving market.

SAN ILDEFONSO, SANTA CLARA, SAN JUAN, TESUQUE, NAMBÉ, AND POJOAQUE PUEBLOS

The Tewa-speaking peoples located in pueblos between Espanola and Santa Fe produce what are probably the Southwest's most famous pottery styles, dramatic shapes decorated with black and red.

San Ildefonso is inseparable from its most famous resident, Maria Martinez (1887–1980)—familiarly called just Maria. Highly romanticized and idealized as an icon in the world of Native American pottery, she is probably the most famous Native American artist of any medium and a legend in her own time. Maria Martinez is credited with single-handedly revitalizing the industry of Native American wares in the Southwest, and she was famous already by 1930, along with her husband, Julian, who decorated many of her pieces. In the early twentieth century she developed the style of shiny black-on-black pottery created by smothering the pot so that no oxygen reaches it. The matte black decoration often includes stylized animals or feathers. Today, many of San Ildefonso's potters produce wares in this style.

Santa Clara counts more than two hundred active potters, which ranks it alongside Acoma as a major pottery capital of the Southwest. Santa Clara artisans have created black pots for many centuries; then added shiny red wares to their repertory in the 1930s. Bear tracks, stylized animals, and other symbolic motifs appear on many vessels. The "wedding vase" with two spouts and one handle symbolizes the union of a bride and groom, who drink water blessed by a holy man from its spouts during the wedding ceremony. The wedding vase originated in Santa Clara, a pueblo that today relies on pottery as its main economic force.

San Juan Pueblo, not far from Taos and Santa Fe, perpetuates a style based on traditional, gray pottery of around 1500 with incised line decoration. Today, the tops and bottoms of the pots are fired with glossy red slip, leaving a raw band across the middle for incised decoration.

Tesuque, Nambé, and Pojoaque constitute minor pottery centers, with artisans who produce human figures and small vessels with primarily black and white decoration of feathers, faces, animals, and geometric patterns.

THE REAL DEAL

Most collectors steer clear of pots that are broken, cracked, or flawed in some way. Fire clouds—black coloration on the outside of the pot—are usually proof that the pot has been fired on an open fire and not in an electric kiln. Some collectors consider fire clouds less desirable, while others seek them out as proof that the object is handmade. Cracks almost always lower the value of the pot.

TAOS AND PICURIS PUEBLOS

Both pueblos high in New Mexico's Sangre de Cristo mountain range are known for pots created with clay incorporated with the glittery mineral mica. Once fired, these vessels take on a shiny, almost metallic appearance that gives them a rich effect. Micaceous ware has been created for centuries, but historians believe this simple style emerged as the dominant one during a period of rebellion on the part of these Tiwa Indians (not to be confused with the Tewa-speaking peoples) against the Spanish in the seventeenth centuries. The pots of Taos and Picuris are simple; the vessels are usually small-scale and utilitarian, with little or no decoration.

In addition to these pottery centers, many other Native American pueblo artisans create pottery of lesser reknown. The ancient pottery traditions of Laguna and Zuni nearly disappeared over the course of the twentieth century, but their traditions were revived during the 1970s. A federal grant to a Laguna potter in 1973 helped the craft flourish. The Hopi, more famous for their katsinam and jewelry, create seed jars, bowls, and other wares from the gray clay around their mesas that turns a honey-apricot color when fired. Their production since the early twentieth century has been dominated by the members of the Nampeyo family, known for their distinctive black decoration.

Fine Native American pottery is widely available in shops across the Southwest. To guarantee that you're getting authentic wares, buy directly from the artisan in the pueblos. Many individual potters post signs in their homes and open them to visitors wishing to learn more and purchase these wares directly from the source; otherwise, buy from a reputable dealer.

TEXTILES

T he Pueblo peoples were the original weavers of the Southwest. In addition to rugs and blankets, they have been weaving clothing, shoes, baskets, and many other objects for thousands of years.

The Navajo, as relative latecomers to the Southwest, probably learned what is now a famous trade from the ancient Pueblo Indians. It seems that Spanish practices had already influenced Navajo weaving by the seventeenth century, especially in the preference for wool over cotton. Navajo weavers made primarily blankets, shirts, and serapes, a special blanket wrap, to wear on cold or wet days.

Throughout the 1800s Navajo textiles were widely traded among Native Americans of all stripes, as well as with Hispanics and Anglos. In fact, the cross-fertilization of ideas among the three cultures is perhaps nowhere better expressed than in textiles. Many historians consider the golden age of Navajo weaving from 1850 to 1870.

THE REAL DEAL

Factors that can increase the value of the rug include the status or notoriety of the weaver, a very fine and tight weave, a more complex and perfect design, wool versus cotton warp threads, and the use of vegetal instead of commercial dyes.

At the end of the nineteenth century, there was a new demand among Anglo traders and collectors for heavy-weight floor coverings. Part of this shift had to do with the availability of commercially made blankets from the Pendleton Company and others, which the Native Americans actively acquired through trade. Anglo owners of several trading posts also encouraged locals to incorporate particular motifs into their weavings to satisfy the demands of their customers. In this way, the trading post system influenced the evolution of Navajo weaving. The most famous examples are the so-called "Ganado red" rugs allegedly developed by John Lorenzo Hubbell of the Hubbell Trading Post. Hubbell created a successful mail-order business by combining the best of traditional Navajo techniques and the most modern materials available.

THE REAL DEAL

Follow your nose to determine if you're looking at an authentic Navajo rug—it should smell like a sheep! Many fakes are made in Mexico, sometimes bearing a label stating that the piece is authentic Navajo. A fake will be lighter in weight, looser in weave, and will have either no animal odor or will smell of chemical dyes.

Before Hispanic settlers introduced sheep to the Southwest in the 1600s, weavers used buffalo hair, horsehair, human hair, or even feathers and plant fibers in their weavings. As was done with baskets, they achieved designs and colorations using the natural dyes of local plant materials.

Eventually many native peoples of the Southwest herded sheep. They began the process of rug making by shearing their animals and washing the wool. Next, they would "card" the wool, or brush it with a special comb to straighten the threads. The weaver then hand-spun the wool using a simple swordlike spindle made of wood. Today, only a small percentage of weavers use hand-spun wool; the vast majority use commercial wool yarn, which allows them to focus their time on weaving the rug rather than on laboriously preparing the material. Dyeing the wool is done at this time if color is desired, either with natural or commercial dyes.

Tools for weaving include forks, and most importantly, a loom. The first Navajo looms were simple devices with two sticks supporting a crosspiece from which the warp—the vertical fibers that anchor the rug—was suspended. Today's looms are still upright but are constructed from milled lumber, which provides more evenness and stability. Weavers weave the weft, the individual threads woven horizontally through the warp, then tamp down each single thread with a special fork designed for that purpose.

This is extraordinarily time-consuming and painstaking work, which in part accounts for the high prices these beautiful works command today. In fact, Navajo textiles rank among the higher-priced Native American crafts because of the labor involved, as well as their long-standing history and reputation for quality. Already in the 1840s traders reported that Navajo serapes (blankets that could be worn and were effective at repelling rain) went for $50 to $60. Today you can expect to spend a few hundred dollars for a small table decoration, and many thousands of dollars for a room-size rug that will last a lifetime.

CHEAT SHEET:
COMMON NAVAJO WEAVING STYLES

• **chiefs**: oldest weaving style known to the Navajo, with colored bands occasionally interrupted by stepped triangles

• **"Ganado red"**: popularized by John Lorenzo Hubbell of the Hubbell Trading Post, these rugs have designs in which red predominates, and include black, white, and gray

• **pictorial**: picture rugs, often with birds and scenes of daily life

• **storm pattern**: shows a central hogan or home, with the four directions or sacred mountains and lightning

• **Teec Nos Pos**: intricate designs showing the influence of Oriental rugs, named for the trading post where the style originated

• **Two Grey Hills**: complex geometric patterns with black, brown, and beige

THE REAL DEAL
Navajo rugs are a big investment, and it pays to carefully examine your potential purchase. You should always spread it out on the floor to check for curling edges, uneven thickness, or asymmetry in the overall rug. Any of these factors may constitute a flaw.

CREAM OF THE CROP
Garland's Navajo Rugs in Sedona (page 110) is one of the industry's most well-respected dealers. At the least, come here to understand what a quality rug looks like, and watch Navajo weavers working the loom.

SAVVY SHOPPER
An authentic Navajo rug can cost thousands of dollars, but with proper care will last a lifetime.

ANGLO-AMERICAN (WESTERN) CRAFTS

T he arrival of "Anglos" to the Southwest in the nineteenth century is usually associated with the arrival of the modern age, with its railroad, commercial goods, industrialization, and mass production. Some contemporary observers believed that Anglo culture spelled the demise of the Hispanic and Native American handmade craft industries, if not their entire civilizations.

However, to subscribe to this view is to neglect the important artisanal traditions that these latecomers to the region crafted in their own right, most of which are associated with cowboy culture—boots, hats, apparel, saddles, gun leather, and other accessories—and their indelible stamp on American culture, especially in the West. Not only are these works important from an art-historical point of view, but they also figure prominently in America's popular imagination and shared memory. Based on both artistic value and cultural importance, they deserve a place alongside the most valued handmade traditions of the Native Americans and Hispanics.

Anglos began trickling to the Southwest in wagon caravans in the 1820s, rolling along the Santa Fe Trail in preliminary trading missions that brought them in contact with Native Americans and Hispanic settlers for the first time. The turbulent mid-century witnessed countless land battles, often bloody, between all three cultures. By the time steam locomotives powered across New Mexico in the late 1870s, Arizona and New Mexico were more firmly in the grasp of the United States government.

Many of the handmade crafts of the Anglo culture are associated with cowboy life. The original cowboys of the nineteenth century traveled from place to place, following the money that came with work on ranches and cattle drives across the Plains and the Southwest. They carried few items with them, nearly all handmade: a pair of cowboy boots, a wide-brimmed hat, saddle and associated tack, chaps, rope, and spurs. Only their simple clothing was likely to be mass-produced and picked up at the dry goods store. Most of these items were based on leather-working and metal-smithing, but innovative craftspeople also began creating beautifully intricate ropes, bridles, belts, hatbands, and other items from horsehair and even cactus fiber.

What many people don't realize is how heavily Western "cowboy" craftsmanship has been influenced by Hispanic culture. Centuries before the first Anglos arrived in the Southwest, Spanish colonists had already established a culture of horsemanship in Mexico, which included often lavish adornments of both horse and rider equal to their wealth, power, and prosperity. Hand-tooled leather saddles, embroidered apparel, and breathtakingly elaborate silver spurs and bits were already well entrenched in the culture by the time Hispanic settlers headed north into modernday New Mexico. Anglo cowboys adapted these forms and invented their own distinctive styles, which, by the turn of the twentieth century, had become standard cowboy gear. Little could anyone guess how, in just a few short decades, the functional cowboy uniform would become America's most beloved fashion statement.

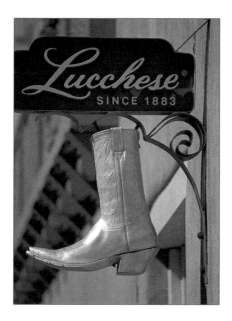

APPAREL

F or sheer razzle-dazzle and pizzazz, it's hard to top the fancy duds that clothing designers have crafted over the last century in the spirit of the Southwest. Fantastic patterns achieved with stitching, embroidery, beadwork, rhinestones, flowers, cacti, animal skulls, and other creative designs have adorned shirts, pants, buckskins, chaps, jackets, and other items for the last century.

Born from necessity, original cowboy wear was much less fancy. Cowboys bought simple clothes at the local dry goods store, and their focus (and their budgets) were on the accessories—boots, hats, chaps, gloves, and other accoutrements. Gloves were important to protect their hands from thorns and rope burns, and leather artisans churned out gloves and gauntlets, gloves with protective sleeves, made of soft tanned hides. Many of the glove artisans were women, experts in sewing and stitching. More elaborate gauntlets were adorned with flowers, stars, or other decorative stitching, and some included fringe or beadwork. Chaps, too, protected the pants and the legs from cold and from chafing against the saddle. They could be covered in woolly sheep fur or untanned cowhides, silver studs and conchas, and stamped leather decoration.

An interesting overlap of apparel styles between Native American, Hispanic, and Anglo cultures evolved. By the mid-1800s, Native Americans could be spotted donning button trousers and shirts with decorative stitching. In turn, many Anglos could be seen on the streets wearing clothes ornamented with traditional Native American motifs and beadwork. Hispanic weavers in Chimayó, New Mexico—long known for making beautiful, quality rugs—began crafting coats and other Western-style apparel with their trademark Spanish-inspired textile designs.

By the late 1800s, sewing machines made it possible to produce garments on a larger scale. Many of the outfits were distributed in mail-order catalogs and shipped across the country. As with cowboy boots, the popularity of Western apparel increased when cowboys hit the big screen. Mexican-style outfits with embroidered floral motifs on the cuffs and along the outer seams of the pants became popular especially after the Hollywood portrayal of cowboys wearing them.

A few key personalities made indelible marks on the evolution of cowboy style. Nathan Turk, a California designer who outfitted John Wayne and other film stars, helped set the taste for elaborate adornments. Later Bobbie Nudie, the original "rhinestone cowboy," became known for designing the most elaborately embellished Western ensembles in his Hollywood design shop. These so-called "Nudie suits" were favorites of Gene Autry and Roy Rogers. Manuel Cuevas, working from Nashville, Tennessee, has continued Turk's and Nudie's traditions to the present day, making costumes for film and rock stars.

In the 1940s, Western-wear manufacturers replaced handwork with machines capable of embroidering designs. Today, only a handful of designers still craft these intricate garments by hand.

THE REAL DEAL

Keep your eye out for these treasures of tailoring at vintage clothing stores, flea markets, and Western shows, but be advised that avid collectors may have already snapped up the most valuable or unique pieces. Western wear from the 1940s and 1950s is particularly collectible.

CREAM OF THE CROP

Liberty Westerns in Santa Fe (page 158) and Rockmount Ranch Wear in Denver (page 132) can turn your dream Western outfit into a reality.

COWBOY BOOTS

I s there any fashion more purely American than cowboy boots? For everyone from real cowboys to Hollywood icons, rock stars, and the average Joe on the street, cowboy boots are synonymous with Western style. The Southwest is the homeland of the cowboy boot, and it's here that a surprising number of the country's best boot makers still craft these amazing shoes by hand.

Of course, American cowboys weren't the first to don boots. Thousands of years of equestrian culture, from Asia's ancient mounted warriors to European nobles, stand behind the horseman's boot. The American West's boot version arose out of necessity, and form necessarily followed function. The original authentic cowboys—those who drove herds of cattle across the central and western states in the 1800s—wore just about any kind of utilitarian boot they could get their hands on, usually flat-heeled, round-toed boots, sometimes surplus from the Civil War. Later they developed and evolved the boot they needed to do their jobs. They enlisted local shoemakers to help them develop the perfect footwear to protect their feet from thorns, rattlesnakes, and weather, and to last a lifetime. American spurs developed as a related craft (see page 91).

The "inventor" of the modern-day cowboy boot is hotly disputed among several important boot makers across the West. What is clear is that by the 1870s the form we know today—higher heel, pointed toe, high shanks (the part that rises from the ankle to the knee)—began to take shape. Some of the early boot-making pioneers developed into larger factories still in operation today. Justin of Fort Worth, Nocona of Nocona, Texas, Tony Lama in El Paso, and Lucchese in San Antonio all trace their origins back a century or more to this key period of cowboy boot development. By the 1920s new styles, materials, and decoration flourished. Boot makers experimented with inlays, decorative stitching, hand-tooling, and exotic skins and colors. Cowboy boots began to catch on around the country.

But the real success of the cowboy boot has little to do with real cowboys and more to do with popular mythology, and later, stars of the silver screen. The lore of the cowboy was romanticized from the late 1800s onward. The popularity of Westerns only served to cement the cowboy boot's popularity across the country. And the boots found new life as a favorite of country crooners and hard rockers—many stars have impressive collections of handmade cowboy boots.

The number of truly excellent boot craftspeople working today is a testament

to the value Americans place on these icons of fashion. Today, as in the past, the artisanal boot maker begins with animal hides. Originally they were crafted from widely available calfskin, and that tradition continues, mostly with calfskins imported from Europe. But the possibilities are endless today, from ostrich to alligator, boar, deer, kangaroo, snake, shark, goat, eel, armadillo, and even bullfrog. Types of hides go in and out of fashion, and they are also affected by the availability of animals. Elephant hides were once highly prized for their durability, but are now banned from the market. Alligator hides, in short supply and loved by many, are by far the most expensive.

Fitting the boot to your individual foot is a high art. In addition to measuring your foot, a good boot maker examines the structure of your feet and makes a last, a wooden model of your individual foot. He or she will also take time to understand where your foot puts pressure on your shoes. While some custom boot makers accept orders via telephone, mail order, or Internet (a few even ship out foam boxes to make an impression of your foot), many handmade boot makers will not sell you a pair of boots unless you appear personally in their shop to be fitted.

Boot factories emerged at the turn of the twentieth century to satisfy the growing demand for cowboy boots. Though their quantities are higher, some of the more commercial boot makers still make quality products and most rely on handicraft for at least part of the production process. Lucchese, Justin, Nocona, and Tony Lama are still producing quality products that rely in part on handmade techniques. A custom boot maker might create ten or twenty pairs of boots a month. Larger boot factories like Justin churn out thousands to satisfy consumers from Tulsa to Tokyo.

═══ CHEAT SHEET: THE COWBOY BOOT ═══

- **piping**: seam down the side of the boot
- **pull strap**: used to pull on boots
- **tongue**: part that extends upward from instep
- **shank**: leather that extends from your ankle to your knee

THE REAL DEAL

Each boot maker has his or her own individual style. Pick what appeals to you, then make a trip to the shop to be fitted. It may seem extravagant to travel from afar, but it is worth making the effort to get a personal fit for an investment of this size.

CREAM OF THE CROP

Many excellent boot makers work from small shops across West Texas. Little's Boots in San Antonio (page 181) is a personal favorite.

SAVVY SHOPPER

Custom-made cowboy boots start at approximately $300 and go up to $2,000 or more depending on materials, style, and the reputation of the maker. A good handmade off-the-shelf pair starts at about $250. Alligator skin boots can cost up to $3,000 or $4,000. If a boot is well made it can last a lifetime.

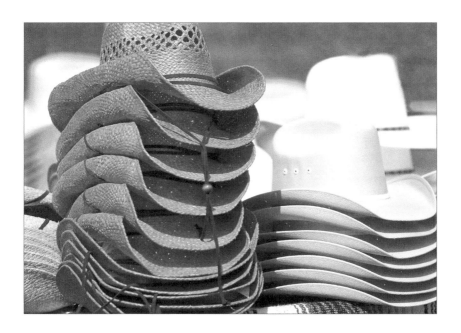

COWBOY HATS

Nothing "tops off" a cowboy's ensemble like the wide-brimmed cowboy hat designed in the nineteenth century to provide shade from the sun as well as enhance the wearer's stature.

Cowboy hats share something in common with the traditional Mexican sombrero, and may owe something to it historically. Texans began donning fancy decorated sombreros at the beginning of the nineteenth century as a popular fashion statement, even as the Mexican-American War raged.

John B. Stetson of the famed Stetson hat company made a foray out west in the 1850s before returning to the East Coast and founding the John B. Stetson Company in 1867. It was the moment when the cattle industry exploded, and Stetson's hats exploded in popularity as well. Renowned for their design and durability, the Stetson name still persists today as a symbol of quality, even though the company is no longer in business. Artisanal hatmakers began fashioning the new popular style out of materials as diverse as the fur from beavers, muskrats, rabbits, and other creatures. Hatbands of ribbon, beading, and other materials were added for effect.

As the Western movie craze waned around the middle of the twentieth century, cowboy hats fell out of fashion, but were revived by the country and rock music industries in the 1970s and 1980s. Today, they have little to do with function and all to do with form.

After a careful measuring of the customer's head, traditional hat making begins with forming the cloth or material around a hat block that replicates the person's head size. Hot irons press the hat and brim into what will become its permanent shape. Steaming can also make the material pliable enough to create subtle creases and upturned edges. Finally, sweatbands inside the hat and hatbands on the outside are stitched on by hand or using a sewing machine.

There are several excellent milliners in the Southwest who specialize in crafting custom hats. Along with cowboy boots, hats constitute a still-thriving handmade industry that brings a rich dimension to today's landscape of Western craftsmanship.

THE REAL DEAL
A reputable hatmaker will spend the time to consult with you on material and style preferences, as well as ensure a custom fit.

CREAM OF THE CROP
Drop into Az-Tex Hats of Scottsdale (page 107) or Nathaniel's of Colorado in Mancos (page 134) for a custom hat that will last forever.

SAVVY SHOPPER
For $100 to $500, you can go home with a handmade hat you'll be proud to wear.

SADDLES

S addles have a history that is as old as riding horses. But saddlery in America owes its heritage specifically to the Hispanic craft tradition. The Spanish conquistadors introduced into the New World an equestrian culture with all of its accoutrements, including the saddles that would prove so essential to American cowboy culture. Early Hispanic settlers brought elaborately decorated saddles with them to the Southwest, and saddles continued to be imported from Mexico to satisfy the needs of the northern colonies. Hispanic craftspeople in New Mexico adapted their craft by learning to make pita, cactus fiber woven into decorative embroidery on leatherwork.

The rising economic need for cowboys in the mid-1800s meant a new demand for saddles and horse tack. Craftsmen met this demand and the new needs of the cowboy—heavier, more robust saddles that weighed in at about forty pounds, and a horn that facilitated roping cattle from horseback.

The saddle tree—the basic skeleton of the saddle—forms the rawhide-covered wooden core onto which the leather is applied. Today, most saddletrees are reinforced with fiberglass to make them less prone to breakage. Leather is glued onto the saddletree, then stamped with decorative patterns when the hide is moistened and supple. The Hispanic models the early Anglo craftsmen followed were intricate and fancy, with elaborate and beautiful leatherwork.

Cowboys turned to saddle makers to personalize their saddles with signature decorations. Roses and other floral motifs—oddly out of keeping with the "manly," rough-and-tumble trade of roping and herding—figured among the most popular decorative motifs; they still do today. Many of these rose designs originated in Spain, but also leaves, sunflowers, and other flora were copied from pattern books and actual saddles the artisans saw or collected. Artisans used hand tools that have been around for centuries—implements such as knives, awls, hammers, mallets, and other stamping tools. Often a saddle workshop employed specialists to stamp decorations into the saddle.

The ranching states of California and Texas emerged as important centers for saddlery, and it is in these two states that you will find today's most accomplished saddle makers. A leather craftsman at heart, the saddle maker was and still is relied upon for related items, including pistol holders, belts, gloves, and other small leather necessities.

THE REAL DEAL

Well into the twentieth century the vast majority of saddles remained hand-made, even with the advent of countless machines that could achieve decora-tive stamping work at a fraction of the time and cost.

CREAM OF THE CROP

Oliver Saddle Shop in Amarillo (page 177) is in its fourth generation of craft-ing handmade saddles.

SAVVY SHOPPER

A good saddle will set you back several thousand dollars. Avid equestrians often start out with a factory saddle but eventually trade up for these beautiful hand-made treasures.

SPURS, BUCKLES, AND OTHER METALWORK

Fastened to boots and often never removed, spurs were standard issue for the original cowboy, helping him guide his horse and stay in the saddle. Spurs have been part of the equestrian outfit for thousands of years, and like the saddle, the basic prototype that entered the American Southwest was Spanish, via Mexico.

These early Hispanic spurs were made of silver or iron, often fancy and elabo-rate in their decoration, sometimes with filigree work and spiky rowels, the starlike spokes that project backward from the spur. Metalsmiths embellished them with engraved flowers, fruits, and other vegetal forms. Plentiful silver mines in Mexico gave them plenty of material. In the Southwest, early settlers used spurs and bridle bits imported from Mexico, or more modest models that smiths could produce from scrap metal—discarded wheel rims, hardware, or farm implements.

From the fancy Mexican prototype, three regional styles of spurs emerged in the Southwest over the course of the nineteenth century: Texas, California, and Plains styles. The Texas style is particularly distinctive, with its large size, silver overlay designs, and often star-shaped rowels. California style is distinguished by more delicate and refined engraving. Plains-style spurs borrow elements from Texas and

California models. The golden age of spur making was approximately 1900 to 1940.

Horse bits as well came from European and Moorish metalsmithing traditions of Spain. All the finest techniques of silversmithing—inlay and overlay, engraving, and other techniques—were utilized in the crafting of these fine early bits. Lizards, snakes, cattle, and other decorative motifs were borrowed from the new world around them. Leather was also incorporated, stamped with the familiar patterns found on saddles, belts, and gun leather. Even after the arrival of Anglos in the mid-nineteenth century and the availability of more commercially produced spurs and bits, Spanish handmade models continued to predominate. Still, Anglo artisans adapted the spurs and bits to use more and chunkier leather and personalized designs.

Today, many spurs are found in private and museum collections, but nice examples can also be found in antique stores. Luckily there are still a few excellent spur craftsmen making these small treasures by hand.

In addition to fancy spurs and bits, metalsmiths began to churn out other cowboy accessories, from belt buckles to bolo ties, conchas, and other jewelry. By the turn of the twentieth century, the production of these items was a large industry, especially in California. Belt buckles in particular play a special role in the history of Western smithing. The tradition of wearing belt buckles as personal adornment

was already common with the Spanish conquistadors who settled in the Southwest: ornamenting themselves and their horses with silver was a sign of wealth and prestige. The Anglo belt-buckle tradition started in the early twentieth century, and the style of wearing a large belt buckle followed from the movies. Belt buckles were also given as rodeo trophies and designed to make highly personal fashion statements.

Most Western belt buckles have a base of sterling silver, which is cut from a sheet to the desired shape and size. The pieces on the back that attach to the belt are then soldered on. Decorative edging is achieved by twisting pieces of metal and soldering them onto the base. In addition, overlays of different metals can achieve decorative effects with images and words. Engraved decorations can be quite elaborate as well. Today, many of the most beautiful and expensive handmade belt buckles are crafted by Native American metalsmiths, often inlaid with turquoise and other stones, or using gold and silver overlays and ornate filigree decoration.

CHEAT SHEET: SPUR STYLES

• **California**: refined, delicate style decorated with engraving

• **Plains**: a mix of California and Texas elements, including large rowels, silver inlay, and wide heel bands

• **Texas**: resemble Mexican ancestors, with chunky heel bands and silver overlay

THE REAL DEAL

Spurs are popular collectibles, and many fanciers specialize in one particular region or maker. Believe it or not, the National Association of Buckle Collectors and the National Bit Spur & Saddle Collectors Association actually exist.

CREAM OF THE CROP

Campbell's Bits and Spurs in Amarillo (page 177) can conjure up any type of spur you can imagine.

SAVVY SHOPPER

You can pick up a quality pair of handmade spurs for a few hundred to a few thousand dollars, depending on the workmanship and the reputation of the maker. Museum-quality antique spurs can fetch up to five figures.

PART II
THE LISTINGS

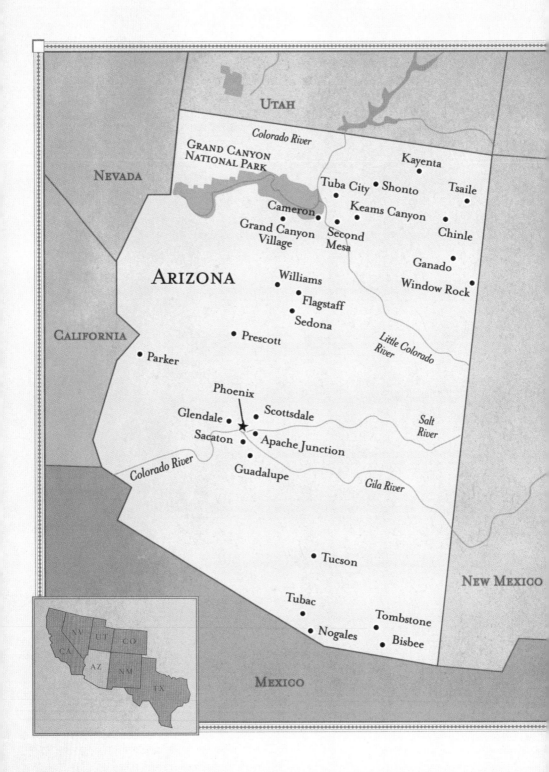

ARIZONA

One of the youngest states (it became the forty-eighth in 1912), Arizona is nonetheless one of the longest-inhabited regions of the country; historians believe it has been continuously populated for some twenty thousand years. Arizona's dramatically diverse climate ranges from desert in the southwest to a green mountain valley through the center and north of the state. The northeast corner is characterized by a vast desert plateau of the Four Corners region with its famous dramatic rock formations.

All three cultures—Native American, Hispanic, and Anglo-American—have exerted a strong presence in Arizona, especially in the realm of craftsmanship. The Native American heritage of Arizona is particularly noteworthy. The Anasazi occupied cliff dwellings and developed an agricultural lifestyle as early as 2000 B.C. The Hopi founded the village of Oraibi around 1200, probably the longest continuously inhabited place in the United States. Today, the northeastern quadrant of the state is home to the Navajo and Hopi nations.

Arizona also became an important center of Hispanic culture after Spanish explorers moved north from Mexico in the mid-sixteenth century. By 1540, the explorer de Cardenas was already marveling at the Grand Canyon, and Spanish missions were established in Native American communities over the course of the seventeenth and eighteenth centuries, notably at Guevavi, Tumacacori, and San Xavier del Bac. Mexico governed Arizona from 1821 until 1853, when it became a U.S. territory.

The 1850s saw the earliest Anglos in Arizona, and for the next thirty years only the hardiest white prospectors, cowboys, explorers, and builders pushed into this territory, still a hotbed of gun battles between the three cultures. By 1881 the railroad roared across Arizona, bringing with it East Coast influences and commercial goods.

Arizona's natural resources have affected the history and development of its craft traditions and industries. Native Americans knew about the turquoise mines for centuries, and pulled the blue stone from the earth as best they could using rudimentary tools; these stones were then fashioned into jewelry and other adornments. The rugged soil was also perfect for crafting pottery. Anglo prospectors uncovered rich deposits of copper, silver, and gold, spawning new industries and towns based around the exploitation of these resources.

The selection of quality crafts in Arizona is staggering. From the treasure trove of Native American resources in the northeastern part of the state to the shopping meccas of Sedona and Scottsdale, and the Hispanic crafts of Tucson and Tubac, visitors will find something to satisfy every desire and budget.

Listings preceded by an asterisk (*) denote my personal favorites.

APACHE JUNCTION

NATIVE AMERICAN

Blue Nugget
4650 North Mammoth Mine Road 45r
(480) 983-6496
www.bluenugget.com

Blue Nugget is an evocative walk into the past, located in the re-created 1890s gold-mining center, Goldfield Ghost Town. This ramshackle remnant of the Old West offers reasonable prices on Native American inlaid watchbands, turquoise jewelry, "liquid silver," and loose turquoise stones.

BISBEE

NATIVE AMERICAN

Bisbee Blue Jewelry
Lavender Pit View Point
(520) 432-5511

Prized for its subtle variations of color, "Bisbee blue" turquoise was mined from the now-defunct local Lavender Pit mine rich with copper deposits. The stones were fitted into traditional Navajo rings, bracelets, necklaces, and other silver adornments. Bisbee Blue Jewelry specializes in the bright stone and every variation of traditional Native American jewelry made with it.

WESTERN

Optimo Custom Hatworks
47 Main Street
(520) 432-4544
www.optimohatworks.com

Make an appointment to be fitted for one of
the finest Panama hats in the country. Hand-
woven in various grades from *selecto* (looser
weave) to *fino fino* (tightest weave), these hats
made by hatmakers in Ecuador are finished
and fitted by Optimo Custom Hatworks. The
shop also carries handcrafted fur hats of
beaver, rabbit, and cashmere. An authentic
Panama hat starts at about $125.

CAMERON

GENERAL CRAFTS

Cameron Trading Post
Highway 89
(928) 679-2231
(800) 338-7385
www.camerontradingpost.com

If you buy something here, you'll pay a
premium for the experience of being in one
of the Grand Canyon area's old traditional
trading posts, established in 1911 on the edge
of the Colorado River Gorge. A gallery displays antique and contemporary Native American pottery, baskets, and rugs from across the
Southwest, including examples from the
Navajo, Hopi, Apache, and Tohono O'odham, as well as Plains Indians beadwork. A
quality selection of antique saddles, bridles,
spurs, and other Western wear may also tempt
your wallet.

NATIVE AMERICAN

Navajo Arts & Crafts Enterprise (NACE)
Highways 89 and 64
(928) 679-2244
www.gonavajo.com

This is the Cameron branch of NACE, established in 1941 as a tribe-endorsed outlet for
Navajo craftspeople. The Cameron store carries a fine array of authentic Navajo crafts
including jewelry, pottery, and rugs. This is a

great place to make purchases if you want to
be sure you're buying a quality, authentic
Indian-made object.

CHINLE

NATIVE AMERICAN

Navajo Arts & Crafts Enterprise (NACE)
Highway 191 and Route 7
(928) 674-5338
www.gonavajo.com

The Chinle branch of NACE sells many of the
same types of objects you find at the other stores
in Window Rock, Kayenta, and Cameron: a
wide selection of high-quality, authentic jewelry,
rugs, pottery, and other crafts at fair, but not
necessarily bargain, prices.

FLAGSTAFF

NATIVE AMERICAN

Museum of Northern Arizona, Museum Shop
3101 North Fort Valley Road
(928) 774-5213
www.musnaz.org

Spend some time with the fascinating and eclectic collections of the Museum of Northern Arizona, which seem to include everything but the kitchen sink—dinosaur bones, minerals, paintings, crafts, and even animal and plant exhibits. Afterward head to the museum shop, which carries authentic Native American baskets, katsina dolls, pottery, Zuni fetishes, and an attractive display of Navajo rugs.

Turquoise Hogan
4 North Leroux Street
(602) 774-0174

Endorsed by the Indian Arts and Crafts Board, this Navajo-owned business carries some particularly nice squash blossom necklaces and bracelets. In addition, peruse the eclectic selection of pottery, beadwork, Hopi katsinam, and other works.

WESTERN

Gene's Western Wear & Shoe Hospital
111 North Leroux Street
(928) 774-3543
(888) 895-9966
www.geneswesternwear.com

If your boots have seen one too many rodeos, take them to Gene's, a Flagstaff fixture for half a century. In addition to its famous cowboy boot repair shop, Gene's also carries a wide selection of fine cowboy hats, boots, and Western wear.

GANADO

NATIVE AMERICAN

*Hubbell Trading Post
Highway 264
(928) 755-3254
www.nps.gov/hutr

Step across the threshold of the Hubbell Trading Post and enter the past. A screen door leads into a dark, old-fashioned general store with creaky, wide-planked floors and merchandise crammed into every corner and suspended from the ceiling. Now operated by the National Park Service, this historic site is the oldest continuously operating Indian

trading post in the Navajo nation. Famed trader John Lorenzo Hubbell took over operation of the trading post in 1878, trading commercial goods with the Navajo in exchange for handmade crafts. Today, prices are competitive on jewelry, baskets, katsina dolls, as well as general provisions. The rug room is one of the most impressive in the country; if you're lucky, you might catch weavers demonstrating their craft on-site. This is an excellent place to see "Ganado red" rugs, a style combining Navajo textile traditions with elements from Oriental rugs that Hubbell himself helped the Navajo develop in the late 1800s to appeal to Anglo collectors.

GILBERT

WESTERN

Tom Paul Schneider
P.O. Box 1239
Pearce, AZ 85625
(520) 824-2010

Make an appointment to visit this professional engraver's workshop, where you can order a special belt buckle or pair of spurs engraved with anything you like from floral motifs to your initials or logo. Tom Paul Schneider knows what he's doing; he was a professional cowboy before turning his interest to metalsmithing.

GLENDALE

NATIVE AMERICAN

Bead Museum, Museum Store
5754 West Glenn Drive
(623) 930-7395
www.beadmuseumaz.org

Bead fans will think they died and went to heaven at Glendale's Bead Museum. This fascinating collection amasses more than a hundred thousand beads and beaded objects from around the world. Many of the exhibitions focus on Native American subjects, including beadwork on clothing and the role of beads in the history of Indian trade. The museum store sells a staggering array of beads of many colors and materials, many of Native American craftsmanship.

GRAND CANYON VILLAGE

NATIVE AMERICAN

Grand Canyon Trading Post
Highway 64
(928) 638-2417

Bypass the T-shirts and hokey coffee mugs and head for the selection of authentic Native American jewelry, pottery, and other crafts on offer at the Grand Canyon Trading Post. The store is located in Tusayan, near the southern entrance to Grand Canyon National Park.

*Hopi House
East of the El Tovar Hotel
(928) 638-2631

Hopi House is one of the more historic shopping experiences of the Southwest. The building was designed in 1905 by Mary E. J. Colter, a pioneering female architect who designed many of the buildings developed by the Fred Harvey Company to serve tourists at the Grand Canyon in the early twentieth century. In this evocative atmosphere of timbered ceilings and corner fireplaces, you'll find a fine array of authentic Native American crafts. The shop is located near the landmark El Tovar Hotel.

Verkamp's
South Rim
(928) 638-2242
(888) 817-0806
www.verkamps.com

Under the watchful eyes of mounted deer, elk, and buffalo heads, you can browse through a large selection of Native American textiles, Hopi katsinam, and fetishes, baskets, and jewelry from many tribes of the Southwest. Verkamp's has been a reliable source of Native American crafts for visitors since it was built at the turn of the twentieth century at the lip of the South Rim.

GUADALUPE

HISPANIC

Mercado Mexico
8212 South Avenida del Yaqui
(480) 831-5925

If you can't get to Mexico, stop by this off-the-beaten-path shop known for its great prices, authentic selection of handcrafted goods from Mexico and Peru, and colorful staff. Look for Talavera pottery, tinware, ceramic tiles, door hardware, Day of the Dead crafts, and many other tiny treasures for just a few dollars. A little rough around the edges, the town of Guadalupe is nonetheless worth a visit to experience its extraordinary mix of Native American and Hispanic cultures. It is located ten miles southeast of Phoenix.

KAYENTA

NATIVE AMERICAN

Navajo Arts & Crafts Enterprise (NACE)
Highway 160
(928) 697-3170
www.gonavajo.com

This is the Kayenta location of Navajo Arts & Crafts Enterprises, a tribe-managed artisan cooperative that offers a decent selection of Navajo crafts at market prices. If you are traveling into Monument Valley from Utah and points north, Kayenta is a convenient stop.

KEAMS CANYON

NATIVE AMERICAN

*McGee's Indian Art
Highway 264
(800) 854-1359
www.ancientnations.com
www.hopiart.com

This is one of the country's oldest and best sources for authentic Hopi crafts, and it is the only traditional trading post on the Hopi reservation. McGee's should top the list for any serious collector of katsina dolls, but it also offers a quality selection of jewelry, rugs, baskets, and pottery. Be forewarned: prices are steep. A fine-quality coiled basket, for example, sells for $500 to $3,000. McGee's occupies a lonely stretch of Highway 264 as it descends into Keams Canyon, just east of the Hopi mesas. The trading post once belonged to John Lorenzo Hubbell—the same man who owned the Hubbell Trading Post in Ganado. In 1937 the McGees, an extended family of Indian traders, took over the store, and it continues to be operated by the family today.

N O G A L E S

W E S T E R N

*Paul Bond Boot Company
915 West Paul Bond Drive
(520) 281-0512
www.paulbondboots.com

An Arizona legend and former rodeo king, Paul Bond got his start crafting custom cowboy boots in the 1920s. Having designed fancy footwear for the likes of John Wayne, Johnny Cash, and Willie Nelson, today this shop of twenty craftspeople on the Mexican border turns out more than a thousand custom-made boots per year. Bond's signatures include tall tops, fancy stitching, and large finger holes for literally pulling yourself up by your bootstraps.

P A R K E R

N A T I V E   A M E R I C A N

Colorado River Indian Tribes Library and Museum, Museum Shop
Corner of Mohave Road and Second Avenue
(928) 669-1335

This nonprofit, tribe-run organization offers a small but quality selection of Navajo rugs, beadwork, katsina dolls, and pottery, as well as a few harder-to-find items such as baby cradle boards and bows and arrows, in its museum shop. The shop is endorsed by the Indian Arts and Crafts Board of the U.S. Department of the Interior.

P H O E N I X

H I S P A N I C

Museo Chicano, Museum Shop
147 East Adams Street
(602) 257-5536
www.museochicano.com

The shop of the Museo Chicano is a great place to stock up on goodies for your Day of the Dead altars as well as other miscellaneous crafts imported from Mexico.

Sueños Latin American Imports
6035 North Seventh Street
(602) 265-3486
www.dayofthedeadmercado.com
www.milagromercado.com

This emporium of crafts from all over Latin America is especially popular with locals every October when *el Día de los Muertos* (the Day of the Dead) rolls around. It carries a huge selection of milagros, as well as lighthearted muertes and other unique pieces of furniture, pottery, textiles, and religious crafts. A few antiques add to an already enticing array of goodies.

N A T I V E   A M E R I C A N

Arizona Tribal Collectors
(602) 769-9190
www.tribalcollectors.com

By appointment only, this twenty-year-old business caters to serious collectors of quality Native American katsinam, pottery, Navajo rugs, and other one-of-a-kind items. It is in the Indian Arts and Crafts Association.

Gilbert Ortega Galleries
122 North Second Street
(602) 265-9923
www.gilbertortega.com

Gilbert Ortega operates a chain of stores in the Phoenix, Scottsdale, and Tempe areas specializing in quality Native American crafts; it is one of the region's more reputable dealers. The Phoenix location, in the Hyatt Regency lobby, carries a fine array of jewelry, pottery, katsinam, and other works.

*Heard Museum, Museum Shop
2301 North Central Avenue
(602) 252-8840
www.heard.org

The Heard Museum shop is an excellent place
to purchase Native American crafts. It's not the
cheapest, but quality and authenticity are guaranteed. After a long search across the Southwest
yielding tacky dream catchers with plastic beads,
I finally located a beautiful one here that my
little son was thrilled to hang by his bedside.
While you're there, be sure to check out the
high-quality exhibitions in this crème de la
crème of Native American institutions.

WESTERN

Az-Tex Hats
10658 North Thirty-second Street
(602) 971-9090
(800) 972-2095

Whether you're a cowboy or a city slicker,
the Phoenix location of the excellent custom
hatmakers Az-Tex Hats can whip up a piece
of fancy custom headgear to suit your style.
There is a store in Scottsdale as well (see
page 107).

Blue Ribbon Custom Tack
15026 North Cave Creek Road
(602) 992-2145
www.blueribbontack.com

Since the 1970s, this saddle-making family
has been turning out quality handmade saddles, in addition to stirrups, spur straps, hal-
ters, saddlebags, belts, and other accessories
suitable for the most discriminating cowboy.

**Desert Caballeros Western Museum,
Museum Shop**
21 North Frontier Street
(928) 684-2272
www.westernmuseum.org

In addition to a mind-boggling array of
trains, train memorabilia, and books on
Western heritage, the store at the Desert
Caballeros Western Museum includes a few
handcrafted Western items suitable for gifts
and as decorative elements for the home.

PRESCOTT

NATIVE AMERICAN

Black Arrow Indian Art
130 West Gurley Street
(928) 776-4092
(800) 621-6668
www.blackarrowindianart.com

A member of the Indian Arts and Crafts
Association, Black Arrow Indian Art offers a
large showroom of Native American jewelry,
as well as more unusual items such as flutes
and reproductions of traditional Indian
apparel.

Smoki Museum, Gift Shop
147 North Arizona Street
(520) 445-1230
www.smokimuseum.org

In an evocative log-and-stone construction,
this small museum of Native American culture
offers quality Zuni fetishes, Tohono O'odham
basketry, silver and turquoise jewelry, pueblo
pottery, and other Native American crafts in
the gift shop.

WESTERN

Merchandise Mart Antiques Mall
205 North Cortez Street
(928) 776-1728
www.merchandise-mart.com

You never know what you'll find in this treasure trove of antiques. On a typical day, you
can rummage through lots of furniture, Western kitsch, and Native American jewelry from
the 1950s and 1960s, but keep your eyes

peeled for handcrafted spurs, saddles, and other Western memorabilia.

P. K. BootMaker
600 Miller Valley Road
(928) 442-1213
www.leatherimages.com

Paul Krause can put just about anything you want on a pair of boots, from your home state's flag to a hidden sheath for a pocket knife. In addition to custom-made boots, Paul also creates other leather items, including wallets, moccasins, belts, and just about anything you can dream up in leather. This leather wizard can also make a pair of beat-up boots look as good as new.

SACATON

NATIVE AMERICAN

Gila River Arts and Crafts Center
Exit 175 at I-10
(520) 315-3411
(480) 963-3981
www.gilaindiancenter.com

At this tribe-run craft cooperative twenty-five miles south of Phoenix, you will find a fine selection of textiles, katsina dolls, beadwork, baskets, jewelry, and more. The store is endorsed by the Indian Arts and Crafts Board of the U.S. Department of the Interior, so you can rest assured that you're buying authentic and quality works.

SCOTTSDALE

This well-heeled suburb of Phoenix is a shopper's paradise, but when it comes to crafts, you have to know where to look. The tourist offices and welcome centers bill Fifth Avenue as a street of artisans, but many of the shops on the street sell works that are run-of-the-mill at best. Better choices abound around Main Street in the Old Town Scottsdale shopping district.

GENERAL CRAFTS

John C. Hill Rare Indian Art
6962 East First Avenue
(480) 946-2910
www.johnhillgallery.com

If you want to be sure that your craft purchase is as unique as it can be, then stop by the John C. Hill gallery. The selection is dominated by Native American antiques—cool traditional katsinam from the 1920s to 1950s, classic Navajo weavings, squash blossom necklaces from the turn of the twentieth century, and other unique pieces. Hill also carries some rare early-nineteenth-century santos by identifiable New Mexican carvers. They are a collector's dream, to be sure, but prepare to pay for uniqueness.

NATIVE AMERICAN

Crazy Horse
7211 East Main Street
(480) 990-8343

This very commercialized store carries some lovely and authentic handmade Native American jewelry.

Faust Gallery
7103 East Main Street
(480) 946-6345
www.faustgallery.com

This upscale gallery is the setting for a variety of exceptional Native American crafts, including rugs, pottery, and jewelry. Many of the works are antiques, from nineteenth-century dolls to vintage Navajo weavings and Native American pottery from the 1880s and 1890s.

Gilbert Ortega's Indian Arts

7252 East First Avenue, (480) 945-1819
7155 East Fifth Avenue, (480) 941-9281

These are two of the larger retail outlets of the Gilbert Ortega chain (see main listing under Phoenix, page 102), with a nice selection of jewelry, pottery, textiles, beaded clothing, and more. Big-ticket items come with certificates of authenticity.

Grey Wolf

7239 East First Avenue
(480) 423-0004
(800) 819-2484

Located in Old Town Scottsdale, the Grey Wolf's friendly and knowledgeable staff can tell you a lot about the store's array of Native American jewelry, pottery, and katsina dolls. Beautiful "war shirts," ranging from $2,500 to $5,000, are bedecked with beads, feathers, and supple leather ornamentation.

The Hopi Shop, Hyatt Regency Scottsdale Resort at Gainey Ranch

7500 East Doubletree Ranch Road
(480) 991-3388

Take a break from sunning yourself at this popular resort to check out the Hopi Shop, which carries a high-quality selection of katsina dolls, textiles, jewelry, and other crafts. Occasionally you can watch craftspeople at work on-site and tour the premier collection of Native American objects on display throughout the hotel. The Hopi Shop is endorsed by the Council for Indigenous Arts and Culture.

King Galleries

7100 Main Street, #1
(800) 394-1843
www.kinggalleries.com

The owner of the King Galleries sits on the board of the directors of the Indian Arts and Crafts Association, which is indicative of the gallery's commitment to high-quality pueblo pottery. Whether your fancy leans toward the geometric black-and-white designs of Acoma, or the black-on-black decorated vessels from Santa Clara, or something else entirely, chances are you can find a quality piece here

and learn more about it than you ever imagined from the knowledgeable staff.

Lovena Ohl Gallery

7144 East Main Street
(480) 946-6746
www.lovenaohl.com

This is one of Scottsdale's most respected dealers in authentic Native American crafts. Expect to pay top dollar for contemporary pueblo ceramics, katsina dolls, unique jewelry, and other miscellaneous handcrafted items.

Old Territorial Shop & Gallery

7077 East Main Street, #7
(480) 945-5432
www.oldterritorialshop.com

A well-regarded Indian arts dealer in business since 1969, Old Territorial offers a spectrum of Native American crafts, from pottery to katsinam, rugs, Maria Martinez–style ceramic wares, and some nice antique beadwork.

Sewell's Indian Arts

7087 Fifth Avenue
(480) 945-0962
www.buyindianarts.com

On a street with more unremarkable Indian arts dealers than you can shake a stick at, Sewell's stands out for its quality inlaid jewelry, eclectic pottery, and handmade belts and buckles with inlaid designs.

Turkey Mountain Traders

7008 East Main Street
(480) 423-8777
www.turkey-mountain.com

This shop is worth a stop for its fascinating array of antique Native American merchandise, from textiles to beadwork and totally unique items. Turkey Mountain specializes in pre-1940 Native American jewelry, and on any given day you might find earrings or a bracelet, pin, bolo, or other gem unlike anything on the street today.

WESTERN

*Az-Tex Hats of Scottsdale
3903 North Scottsdale Road
(480) 481-9900
www.aztexhats.com

It's fun to try on the myriad styles of artisanal cowboy and Panama hats in this Scottsdale shop. Az-Tex makes all its own hats and will custom make a model fit just for your head. A friendly Australian shepherd will shadow you as you browse the hand-tooled belts, bags, and accessories inside the Old Town Scottsdale location. Az-Tex Hats also has a store in Phoenix (see page 103).

Porter's of Scottsdale
3944 North Brown Avenue
(480) 945-6182

This store offers one of Scottsdale's best selections of quality cowboy boots that use both handmade techniques along with more modern forms of manufacturing, including Lucchese and Justin lines. It also carries other Western wear, from belts to shirts, jackets, and jeans.

Saba's Western Store
3965 North Brown Avenue,
(480) 947-7664
7254 Main Street, (480) 949-7404
www.sabaswesternwear.com

With several locations around Phoenix and Scottsdale, including these two locations in Old Town Scottsdale, Saba's is one of the area's more well-respected commercial Western-wear establishments. If you're looking for a good selection of men's and women's hats, boots, clothing, and accessories, this is a good bet. Saba's represents many of the quality larger-scale boot-making companies, including Lucchese.

SECOND MESA

The center of Hopi life, Second Mesa has the majority of craft retail outlets in the Hopi Nation. For an insider's orientation to the Hopi lands, contact Bertram Tsavadawa at (928) 306-7849; he is a friendly and knowledgeable guide who can tell you everything you ever wanted to know about the Hopi, from their crafts to ancient petroglyphs in the area.

NATIVE AMERICAN

Honani Crafts-Gallery
Highway 264, west of the junction with Highway 87
(520) 737-2238

This Hopi-run operation offers up a nice selection of the tribe's overlay silver jewelry, katsinam, baskets, and pottery. It also carries works from other tribes, notably Santo Domingo jewelry, Navajo textiles, and Zuni fetishes.

Hopi Arts & Crafts Silver Craft Cooperative Guild
Highway 264
(928) 734-2463

Alongside the Hopi Cultural Center, this co-op serves as the central organization for Hopi silversmiths. The opening hours are inconsistent, but if you're lucky enough to find it open, this is a great place to buy the characteristic Hopi overlay silver jewelry.

Hopi Cultural Center
Highway 264
(928) 734-2401
www.hopiculturalcenter.com

The heart of the Hopi reservation, the Hopi Cultural Center occupies the apex of Second Mesa. At the Arts & Crafts shops here you can buy crafts representative of the Hopi: katsina dolls, pottery, coiled baskets, and silver overlay jewelry.

Tsakurshovi
East of the Hopi Cultural Center
(928) 734-2478

Originators of the local "Don't Worry Be Hopi" T-shirt craze, this small shop carries what is probably the reservation's best selection of Hopi baskets, including some woven by the owner's wife, Janice Day, a noted basket weaver. You will also find katsina dolls and traditional Hopi jewelry.

SEDONA

Tlaquepaque Village is a great place to start crafts shopping in Sedona, a mecca of red rocks and relaxation. This lovely, Mediterranean-style pedestrian district is full of quality shops with handmade goods from all three traditions. Though some locals pronounce Tlaquepaque as "to lock your pocket," you can actually find some decent values on quality crafts if you know where to look.

GENERAL CRAFTS

Cocopah Beads
Tlaquepaque Village
(928) 282-4928
www.beadofthemonthclub.com

Though this funky shop carries beads from all over the world, there are a few nice samples of work from Native American and other southwestern artisans. Avid beaders can sign up for the bead-of-the-month club, and sample its selection by mail order all year long.

Esteban's
Tlaquepaque Village
(928) 282-4686

This tasteful contemporary pottery collection includes works by Native American potters.

*Gifted Hands
Tlaquepaque Village
(928) 282-4822

Gifted Hands displays Sedona's best selection of contemporary crafts and is a particularly good source for men's gifts such as handcrafted knives with carved handles. Native American baskets, corn maidens, and other unique items round out the selection.

Isadora Handweaving Gallery
Tlaquepaque Village
(928) 282-6232
www.mckeowngalleries.com

This cozy shop is full of hand-knitted sweaters, scarves, and other accessories, and is a great place to find baby gifts.

HISPANIC

Cosas Bonitas de Mexico
Tlaquepaque Village
(928) 204-9599
www.mexidona.com

Beautiful Mexican ceramics, retablos, bultos, and other religious and decorative works line the shelves of this small, colorful shop on one of Tlaquepaque's most picturesque plazas. Beware the baskets made in Pakistan.

El Picaflor Arts and Crafts
Tlaquepaque Village
(928) 282-1173
www.elpicaflor.com

El Picaflor specializes in Peruvian crafts, especially the impressive and intricate retablos, wooden altarlike contraptions with doors that open to reveal humorous scenes of village life rather than religious subjects. Tiny plaster figures portray patrons of local bars, as well as street tradesmen, from fruit vendors to mask makers. Day of the Dead characters also grace the shelves of this small, bright shop on the upper level.

*Mexidona
1670 West Highway 89A
(928) 282-0858
www.mexidona.com

The owners of Cosas Bonitas de Mexico (see page 108) also run this ample Hispanic furniture and decorative showcase. The focus here is on the handcrafted, with truly unique and beautiful pieces from chests, sideboards, religious art, mirrors with tin frames, wrought iron candlesticks, and Talavera pottery. Prices are reasonable considering the quality and uniqueness.

Nectar
Tlaquepaque Village
(928) 203-4749

I picked up a special bulto from Guatemala in this shop, which offers jewelry, tinware, retablos, and other handcrafted works from all over Latin America. Buyer beware: A few Pakistani baskets are thrown into an otherwise authentic Latin American craft inventory.

NATIVE AMERICAN

Blue-Eyed Bear
299 North Highway 89A
(928) 282-1158
www.blueeyedbear.com

For those whose taste leans more toward the contemporary, Blue-Eyed Bear specializes in Native American jewelry with its roots in tradition but with a more contemporary spirit. Silver bracelets and pendants of silver inlay are particularly well done.

*Garland's Indian Jewelry
Indian Gardens
3953 North Highway 89A
(928) 282-6632
www.garlandsjewelry.com

The Garlands of rug fame (see following entry) also run Sedona's premier Native American jewelry store, full of the best traditional designs of the Native American Southwest. Garland's is a quality, reputable dealer and you can be assured of authenticity and quality, as well as excellent service.

*Garland's Navajo Rugs
411 Highway 179
(928) 282-4070
www.garlandsrugs.com

This store has one of the Southwest's largest selections of high-quality Navajo rugs. Ask the helpful staff to demonstrate the hallmarks of an authentic Navajo rug, and browse through the hundreds of options suspended from the ceiling racks. The back room showcases antique pottery, baskets, and rugs that appeal especially to collectors. Native American weavers often work on the premises, so this is an excellent opportunity to watch this ancient craft in action. Prices are commensurate with the quality and service you'll get at this Sedona institution.

Gordon Wheeler's Trading Post
201 Highway 179
(928) 282-4255

Although it's a rather hokey takeoff on the historical trading post, this shop has an Indian pawn room that is one of the more interesting treasure troves of antique turquoise jewelry in the area.

Hoel's Indian Shop
9589 North Highway 89A
(928) 282-3925
www.hoelsindianshop.com

Hoel's is on a stretch of road in the scenic Oak Creek Canyon area ten miles north of Sedona. Offered is a variety of Native American katsina dolls, pottery, jewelry, and other works. If you need a place to stay, check out Hoel's rustic log cabins just down the road.

The Humiovi
247 North Highway 89A
(928) 282-5259

Among more touristy kitsch that, strangely, has nothing to do with Native Americans are a few quality pieces of Hopi jewelry.

*Kópavi International
Garland Building
411 Highway 179
(928) 282-4774
(877) 456-7282
www.kopaviinternational.com

Whether you have a passing or passionate interest in Hopi craftsmanship, chances are you'll find something to strike your fancy in this quality store. Although this shop special-izes in Hopi silver overlay and gold jewelry, it also carries beadwork, moccasins, headdresses, and other interesting objects all beautifully arranged in glass display cabinets. The setting is elegant: crystal chandeliers, fine rugs, and lovely woodwork ornament this space on the upper level above Garland's Navajo Rugs.

Ninibah
Tlaquepaque Village
(928) 282-4256

You're likely to find the owners trading with their Native American suppliers in this bou-tiquelike shop in Tlaquepaque. Prices are somewhat expensive, but you can find a few quality pieces of jewelry and Navajo weavings.

Turquoise Buffalo
252 North Highway 89A
(888) 448-2994
www.turquoisebuffalo.com

Turquoise Buffalo carries jewelry crafted with the unusual "white turquoise"—a very light-colored turquoise that is rare. Sometimes pure white and sometimes streaked with blue, white turquoise mixed with traditional stones combines to create fabulous bracelets, neck-laces, and other pieces. Turquoise Buffalo can custom design a piece just for you. While this is mostly a jewelry dealer, you can also pick up Native American pottery, katsina dolls, and clothing with colorful beadwork. Turquoise Buffalo is located on the upper level of Sinagua Plaza off of Highway 89A.

Turquoise Tortoise Contemporary Gallery
101 North Highway 89A
(928) 282-6018
www.turqtortpinonpt.com

Located inside the Hyatt Hotel, Turquoise Tortoise hosts interesting special exhibitions and receptions of Native American artisans. The gallery carries colorful handmade jewelry and sculpture, and other works by Native American artisans of various tribes.

Uniquely Southwest
320 North Highway 89A
(928) 282-2339
www.uniquelysw.com

This small shop specializes in the native Zapotec weavings from Mexico, including rugs, pillowcases, mats, and other decorative items. Look for the rugs draped over the balcony near the Turquoise Buffalo (see page 110).

WESTERN

Bob McLean Custom Boot Maker
40 Soldier Pass Road
(928) 204-1211

A premier maker of quality handmade cowboy boots in an array of leathers and designs, this artisan's shop is a division of the Paul Bond Boot Company. Also check out the belts executed in exotic leathers.

Cahill Leather Company
235 North Highway 89A, Suite #1
(928) 282-0065
www.cowboycorral.com

Run by the proprietors of the Cowboy Corral (see following entry), this shop in the arcade showcases a small but high-quality selection of boots, bags, and leather accessories, many displaying fine hand-tooling.

*Cowboy Corral
219 North Highway 89A
(928) 282-2040
(800) 457-2279
www.cowboycorral.com

If you want to beef up your wardrobe of Western wear, you can't get much more authentic than this. True cowboy gear, from holsters to chaps, spurs, belts, Victorian ladies' corsets, rifles, and beaver hats, lines the shelves and racks of this unique shop. Some are antiques, others are reproductions. Cowboy Corral also carries a huge selection of cowboy books and magazines, so you can read up on all the gear and accessories no real cowboy can live without.

Joe Wilcox Stagecoach Trading Post
300 North Highway 89A, Suite #2
(928) 282-1701

A small but fine selection of Western wear characterizes this shop. Lucchese cowboy boots and hand-tooled leather bags for around $100 are the highlights, but there is also a nice selection of cowboy hats, jewelry, and bolo ties.

Up West Leather, Tack & Feed
470 North Highway 89A
(928) 204-1341
(877) 204-1341
www.upwestleather.com

A plethora of leather goods from horse bridles to saddles, hand-tooled belts and bags, and other Western accoutrements decorate the interior of this cozy Sedona shop. Friendly service tops off the experience. The decorative pillows made of fur are nice, but some are made in China or Brazil. Check the tags.

SHONTO

NATIVE AMERICAN

Shonto Trading Post
East of Highway 98
(928) 672-2320

This historic trading post appears against a backdrop of desolate red rocks in the Navajo nation's Shonto Canyon. The original structures were destroyed by fire, but today a ramshackle building houses some nice Navajo textiles as well as the quality saddle blankets that have brought the trading post renown through the years.

TOMBSTONE

WESTERN

Tombstone Mercantile Company
720 East Fremont Street
(520) 457-1489
www.tombstonemercantileco.com

You might just find a treasure in this expansive jumble of antique Western memorabilia and cowboy goodies from the past—clothing, riding gear, cowboy movie memorabilia, even old wagons and vintage cars.

William Brown Holster Company
302 East Fremont Street
(520) 457-9208
(800) 337-5250
www.wmbrownholster.com

This leather wizard crafts historically accurate reproductions of holsters, saddlebags, spur straps, chaps, and other leather accessories befitting the most authentic cowboy. A fascinating taste of the past!

TSAILE

NATIVE AMERICAN

Hatathli Gallery
Navajo Community College
Intersection of Navajo routes 12 and 64
(928) 724-6654

This nonprofit organization on the Navajo reservation is endorsed by the Indian Arts and Crafts Board. The work of many reservation artisans is shown in an ever-changing display of handcrafted Navajo jewelry, beadwork, rugs, and other crafts.

TUBA CITY

NATIVE AMERICAN

Tuba City Trading Post
Intersection of Monabe and Main streets
(928) 283-5441

You can often hear the Navajo native tongue in this historic trading post on the western edge of the Navajo reservation. Trading post owners act as jacks-of-all-trades, filing taxes, selling money orders, cashing checks, and facilitating a myriad of other transactions for their Navajo neighbors. Among a few touristy items you can find some quality jewelry and rugs. Check out the reproduction hogan, or traditional Navajo dwelling, on the trading post grounds.

TUBAC

Arizonans refer to Tubac as the Sedona of Southern Arizona for its artists' colony, which is home to hundreds of painters, sculptors, and artisans of all stripes. Located forty miles south of Tucson near the Mexican border, Tubac boasts close to a hundred galleries and artists' studios; it is a great place to find traditional crafts.

HISPANIC

Accent on Mexico
19 Tubac Road
(520) 398-2828

Hand-hammered copper decorative accents, Talavera sinks and outdoor pottery, rustic furniture, and hand-painted wooden critters round out this bonanza of crafts from Mexico and other Latin American countries.

El Rincon
12 Plaza Road
(520) 398-3999

Wrought iron accent furniture, tin-framed mirrors, colorful pottery, and hand-hewn wooden furniture from Mexico are among the offerings at this shop. A constant supply of different Day of the Dead wares will augment your collection.

La Paloma de Tubac
1 Presidio Drive
(520) 398-9231

This is Tubac's largest selection of south-of-the-border handcrafted items, featuring works from Mexico to Guatemala and Peru. Whether you're seeking santos, pottery, tile work, or a unique muerte to round out your Day of the Dead collection, chances are you'll find it in this Old Town store. Prices are reasonable and shopping here is a fun experience.

La Piñata
18 Tubac Road
(520) 398-2060

Displayed among more commercialized decorative items are a few quality pieces, including Mexican tinware, furniture, and jewelry.

NATIVE AMERICAN

Old Presidio Traders
27 Tubac Road
(520) 398-9333
www.oldpresidiotraders.com

Look beyond the T-shirts and other souvenirs to find a few quality handcrafted silver and gold jewelry pieces, baskets, katsina dolls, and pueblo pottery. The store carries a fascinating treasure trove of Indian pawn jewelry and is an active member of the Indian Arts and Crafts Association.

TUCSON

This city boasts one of the best selections of handmade goods in the Southwest. Most of its shops are spread out across the urban sprawl, so be prepared to drive around to hit all of Tucson's handcrafted hot spots.

GENERAL CRAFTS

Del Sol
435 North Fourth Avenue
(520) 628-8765

While the quality of the works in this shop is disappointing overall, it admirably attempts to assemble crafts from Hispanic, Native American, and Western traditions under one roof.

Patania's Sterling Silver Originals
174 East Tool Street
(520) 795-0086
www.patanias.com

The Patanias are one of the country's premier families of metal artisans. Frank Patania opened the Thunderbird Shop in 1937, and his works in silver and gold gained him a national reputation. Samuel Patania continues the tradition; he is the third generation of artisans in his family, which is known for quality workmanship and gorgeous silver items.

HISPANIC

Antiqua de México
3235 West Orange Grove Road
(520) 742-7114

The large warehouse-style showroom carries a fabulous array of handcrafted Mexican imports, from colorful ceramics to tinware, pewter, furniture, religious works, and wrought iron.

*Aquí Esta
204 South Park Avenue
(520) 798-3605

One of the Southwest's best sources for authentic Hispanic home decorative elements, Aquí Esta carries rustic hand-painted furniture, ceramic tiles and sinks, wrought iron door pulls, and beautiful architectural woodwork.

TRAWLING TUCSON'S CRAFTS

Tucson is vast and spread out across the desert, but concentrations of craftspeople can be found in these enclaves:

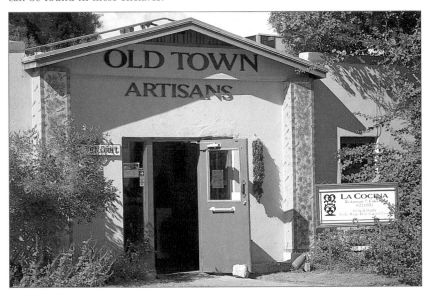

· North Fourth Avenue   · Lost Barrio Shopping District   · Old Town Artisans

Unique custom-made kitchen cabinets are a specialty. This wonderland of craftsmanship is located in the Lost Barrio Shopping District, and its warehouse setting allows for one of the area's largest selections of Hispanic crafts.

Carlos Diaz Silversmiths
2815 North Campbell Avenue
(520) 327-8113
www.carlos-diaz-silversmiths.com

Make a foray into the world of silversmithing in this friendly, family-run shop. From jewelry to stunningly simple silver and gold candlesticks, vessels, and dinnerware, this warm retail workshop has been churning out quality merchandise since Carlos Diaz emigrated from Colombia to Tucson in the 1950s. Today, you can often find one of the Diaz family members working on-site on one of the shop's signature pieces.

Casa Mexicana
143 South Park Avenue

Though at first this seems like a commercial furniture and interior design showroom, Casa Mexicana offers some very fine custom furniture from armoires to sideboards, much of it hand-painted with southwestern motifs. Look for Casa Mexicana across from the main stores in the Lost Barrio Shopping District.

Colonial Frontiers
244 South Park Avenue
(520) 622-7400
www.colonialfrontiers.com

In a cramped but evocative showroom, Colonial Frontiers showcases an eclectic mélange of handcrafted furniture and decorative items from Mexico, Peru, Ecuador, and farther-flung countries like Indonesia. The selection is small but the quality is high. The ceramics in particular are excellent.

*La Hormiga Blanca
340 North Fourth Avenue
(520) 628-4160
www.lahormigablanca.net

In one of Fourth Avenue's largest retail spaces, La Hormiga Blanca, or "white ant," is chock-full of rustic furniture, wrought iron hardware, Talavera sinks, bowls full of milagros, and decorative items. I purchased a rustic Mexican cross encrusted with milagros for $35, a good value considering its uniqueness.

Méjico Maxico Imports
278 East Congress Street
(520) 884-5295

A relative newcomer to Tucson's downtown shopping scene, Méjico Maxico assembles a fine collection of pewter wares, something you don't often find in other Tucson shops hawking Hispanic crafts. There are also a few pieces of colorful Talavera pottery.

Mi Casa Mexican Extravaganza
3248 East Grant Road
(520) 322-8196

"Mexican extravaganza" sums up this large retail space on a prime shopping street, which carries lovely examples of Mexican imports from rustic pine furniture to ceramics and religious items suitable for home decoration.

Morning Star Antiques
2000 East Speedway Boulevard
(520) 881-3060
www.morningstartraders.com

Morning Star Antiques and its sister store, Morning Star Traders (see page 117), are among Tucson's most venerable institutions selling southwestern crafts. Morning Star Antiques specializes in Spanish colonial and Mexican furniture and decorative elements, with an impressive selection of antique santos, rustic chests, tables, and pottery. Prices are steep, but the quality of the antique furnishings is high.

Picante Designs
2932 East Broadway Boulevard
(520) 320-5699

Bypass the more touristy clothing items to check out this store's nice selection of retablos painted on tin.

*Rústica
200 South Park Avenue
(520) 623-4435

Along with Aquí Esta (see page 113), Rústica makes Tucson's Lost Barrio Shopping District one of the best places in the Southwest to buy authentic handmade Mexican furniture and decorative crafts. Among the many unique items are ornate armoires with hand-painted saints and angels, and a fine selection of Talavera pottery.

Rústicos Méxicanos
218 North Fourth Avenue
(520) 882-0827

I purchased a giant, hand-hewn block of wood with two dozen holes for candles for the center of my dining table. It's this type of unique, rustic decorative craft—including benches, chairs, and wrought iron accessories—that characterizes the inventory of Rusticos Mexicanos, located in Tucson's funky Fourth Avenue shopping district.

Spanish Cross Trading Co.
2629 East Broadway Boulevard
(520) 322-5383

For unique Spanish colonial antiques, this is one of Tucson's best stops. The tiny retail space brims with battered doors with peeling turquoise paint, hand-tooled leather saddles, and gorgeous antique furniture. Prices are reasonable considering the uniqueness of the items.

Tarahumara Imports
417 North Fourth Avenue
(520) 903-1463

Tarahumara's Fourth Avenue location is a tiny treasure trove jam-packed with unique hand-crafted Hispanic furniture and home acces-sories. This shop has some of the best values in Tucson, even carrying antique and con-temporary oil paintings for under $200.

Tolteca Tlacuilo
186 North Meyer Avenue
(520) 623-5787
(888) 779-8081
www.toltecatlacuilo.com

Located in the enclave of Old Town Artisans, this shop carries Day of the Dead crafts, Mex-ican pottery, and a wealth of other Hispanic goodies.

Zócalo
3016 East Broadway Boulevard
(520) 320-1236

One of the city's newest additions to a market already teeming with quality Spanish colonial furniture and decorative items, Zócalo offers a nice selection of Mexican furniture, chan-deliers, and other decorative items.

NATIVE AMERICAN

*Bahti Indian Arts
4280 North Campbell Avenue, Suite 100
(520) 577-0290
www.bahti.com

Located in St. Philip's Plaza, a posh shopping district on the north side of town, Bahti is my pick for Tucson's best selection of authentic Native American crafts; the merchandise is lovely. Beautifully arranged in a gallery setting are turquoise jewelry, katsina dolls, and other crafts. The Native American sales staff is informative, and frequent demonstrations and lectures by prominent Native American craftspeople enrich your appreciation. Bahti Indian Arts was founded in 1952 by Tom Bahti, and is now run by his son, Mark.

Desert Son Indian Art
4759 East Sunrise Drive
(520) 299-0818
www.desertson.com

Located in the tony Catalina Foothills section of Tucson, Desert Son has a quality collection of Hopi katsinam, hand-stamped belts and buckles, moccasins, jewelry, and more. Pen-dants and bracelets with multicolored stones, wildly popular at the moment, are particularly well done.

*Grey Dog Trading Co.
2970 North Swan Road, #138
(520) 881-6888
www.greydogtrading.com

Grey Dog Trading is one of Tucson's most well-respected Indian art dealers, located in an upscale, colorful adobe shopping complex. The inventory is limited but hand-selected, and includes works by tribes of the Southwest, Plains, and Pacific Northwest. The drums are particularly cool.

Kaibab Moccasins
227 East Valencia Road
(520) 573-0595
(888) 524-2227

Handcrafted moccasins in Native American styles are the main attraction in this established shop. Buy off the shelf, or order a pair of custom moccasins. People who know these shoes swear by them for comfort and durability.

Mac's Indian Jewelry
2400 East Grant Road
(520) 327-3306

On a street known for its antique shops, Mac's stands out with its bright pink adobe building. Display cases house an impressive selection of authentic Navajo and Hopi jewelry, as well as dream catchers, rugs, and Hopi katsinam. Mac's will also repair silver jewelry.

Medicine Man Gallery
7000 East Tanque Verde Road
(520) 722-7798
www.medicinemangallery.com

Next door to his Museum of the West, J. Mark Sublette and the Medicine Man Gallery carry fine art as well as antique Native American crafts, including beadwork, baskets, textiles, pottery, and jewelry. The store and museum are located in a commercial strip east of downtown.

Morning Star Traders
2020 East Speedway Boulevard
(520) 881-2112
www.morningstartraders.com

In its evocative, beamed gallery, Morning Star Traders assembles a fine collection of Native American textiles, baskets, pottery, and jewelry—some antique, some new. The store's most impressive space is the rug room, where traditional rug styles from across the Southwest are artfully displayed. One of the city's most reputable stores, it has been in business for thirty years.

Oriental Rug Repair Company
245 South Plumer Avenue, #15
(520) 790-1871
www.navajorugrepair.com

If your "Ganado red" has seen better days, take it down to the Oriental Rug Repair Company, which specializes in repairing and stabilizing Navajo rugs. Rug conservators will carefully examine and clean the rug, then make repairs using any one of thousands of colored wool yarns in the shop's inventory

that match the original colors. It's an excellent place to go to protect your investment.

*San Xavier Mission
San Xavier del Bac Mission
(520) 294-2624
www.sanxavierdelbac.org

A fascinating melding of Hispanic and Native American cultures appears in the desert on the southern fringes of Tucson. Spanish Franciscan missionaries set up an impressive mission to convert the local Tohono O'odham people in 1700. Despite this outside influence, the Tohono O'odham have retained their indigenous craft traditions. The tribe is known for its simple baskets made of yucca and horsehair, as well as "friendship pots" with figures encircling the vessels in a sign of unity of peoples around the world. The mission's arts and crafts center has a handful of shops selling authentic wares at reasonable prices. I paid $48 for an eight-inch basket, substantially less than I would have paid for a comparable basket in Navajo or Hopi country. Friendship pots run $15 to $200, depending on the size. The museum store alongside what is considered by many to be the most beautiful church in America also carries authentic Native American wares.

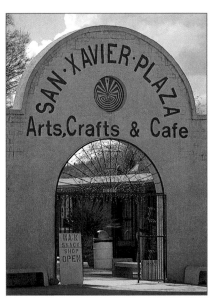

Talawepi Gallery
545 North Fourth Avenue

This Indian-owned gallery on artsy Fourth Avenue carries a limited selection of high-quality, high-priced handcrafted items of the Navajo, Hopi, Isleta, and Tohono O'odham peoples, among other groups. A small glass curio carries Hopi katsinam in the $2,000 price range.

Tucson Museum of Art, Gift Shop
140 North Main Avenue
(520) 624-2333
www.tucsonmuseumofart.org

Among contemporary crafts and more commercial gift items, the Tucson Museum of Art shop has a few traditional, high-quality Native American pots, baskets, and katsina dolls. The museum sponsors a holiday craft market in late November, featuring the work of some of the region's best weavers, potters, and woodworkers.

Turquoise Door
4330 North Campbell Avenue
(520) 299-7787
www.turquoisedoorjewelry.com

Located in St. Philip's Plaza near Bahti Indian Arts, Turquoise Door carries a nice selection of jewelry crafted by Navajo, Hopi, and other Native American artisans. Many of the pieces are more contemporary than traditional in spirit—good for those who want quality jewelry but want to depart from traditional Native American forms.

WESTERN

*Arizona Hatters
2790 North Campbell Avenue
(520) 292-1320
www.azhatters.com

A Tucson institution, this is the place to go for a classic, custom-fitted Stetson. Arizona Hatters has earned a reputation for hat fitting and shaping, using special lathe and flange machines that have created headgear for more than a hundred years and for many thousands of happy hat wearers.

Petroglyphs Furniture, Lighting, and Accents
141 South Park Avenue
(520) 628-4764

Across from the Lost Barrio warehouse, Petroglyphs specializes in handmade wrought iron and rustic brass home accessories.

Stewart Boot Company
30 West Twenty-eighth Street
(520) 622-2706

In one of Tucson's seedier parts of town, in perhaps its seediest building, is one of America's most well-respected makers of handcrafted cowboy boots. Stewart boots are a good value considering their high quality—only $255 for boots off the shelf, or $285 for a made-to-measure pair ready within ninety days.

Western Lifestyle Furniture
2330 and 2354 East Broadway Boulevard
(520) 629-9979
www.countrywesternlifestyle.com

If you have a hankering for wagon-wheel furniture, a cowhide chair, or a deer antler chandelier, Western Lifestyle Furniture can make your dreams a reality. Chairs made of rough-hewn limbs and wagon-wheel benches sit alongside many one-of-a-kind items in this imaginative showroom. Custom order a piece to suit your own taste.

WILLIAMS

NATIVE AMERICAN

Pueblo Indian Gallery
202 West Route 66
(928) 635-4966
www.puebloindiangallery.com

A large assortment of Hopi, Navajo, and Zuni jewelry, pottery, and other works are artfully displayed in an imposing historic building that once served as the Citizen's Bank.

WESTERN

Old Trails Blacksmith & Hardware
321 East Route 66
(928) 635-4512

On Williams's touristy Old West Main Street, this shop offers a fascinating glimpse into the world of the blacksmith. Watch these old-style craftsmen hammer works of beauty on a hot forge.

WINDOW ROCK

NATIVE AMERICAN

Navajo Arts & Crafts Enterprise (NACE)
Highway 264 and Route 12
(928) 871-4090
www.gonavajo.com

Window Rock is the capital of the Navajo nation, and you can rest assured that you are getting quality, authentic goods at Navajo Arts & Crafts Enterprises. Located alongside the Navajo Nation Museum, this non-descript building houses a great selection of Navajo jewelry, including exceptional squash blossom necklaces and bracelets. The basket and rug selections are slim, but the jewelry selection is among the best in the area.

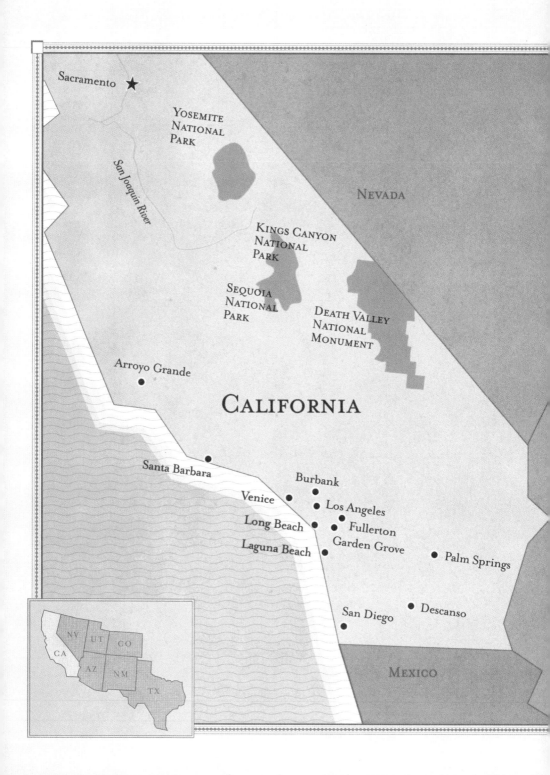

Sacramento ★

YOSEMITE
NATIONAL
PARK

San Joaquin River

NEVADA

KINGS CANYON
NATIONAL
PARK

SEQUOIA
NATIONAL
PARK

DEATH VALLEY
NATIONAL
MONUMENT

Arroyo Grande

CALIFORNIA

Santa Barbara

Burbank

Venice

Los Angeles

Long Beach

Fullerton

Laguna Beach

Garden Grove

Palm Springs

San Diego

Descanso

MEXICO

NV
UT
CO
CA
AZ
NM
TX

SOUTHERN CALIFORNIA

A vast variety of Native American peoples once inhabited what is now California, some as long ago as 10,000 BC. These hunting, fishing, and gathering communities relied on handmade goods to support their way of life, notably a wide variety of basket types for gathering, cooking, and storing food, as well as ceremonial costumes and handmade boats.

Spanish explorers first reached California by boat from Mexico, and over the course of the 1700s they organized significant missions along the coast from San Diego northward, attempting to colonize the land and govern the natives. In 1825 California joined the Mexican Republic, now independent of Spain. As in New

Mexico, these Hispanic settlers brought both Old World and New World craft traditions with them, and those that were required to survive in the colonies—wrought iron, religious goods, basic furniture—are the ones that thrived in California. California still boasts a rich Hispanic culture and population, which continues to express itself in craft production, notably in and around San Diego.

In the early 1840s, the first significant Anglo population arrived in California. Their arrival corresponded with the discovery of gold in several key locations. After the bitter Mexican-American War, California became a U.S. territory in 1848 and a state in 1850. Now with California firmly within the U.S.'s reach, a flood of immigrants from all over the land poured into the West Coast to prospect for gold. Once the Gold Rush ended in the 1850s, silver mining overtook it as California's key industry, and metalsmiths remained in high demand. With an active ranching culture, the "California spur" developed as a distinct type of boot spur around the turn of the twentieth century to meet the needs of cowboys and ranchers who tied their lives and livelihoods to southern California.

Listings preceded by an asterisk (*) denote my personal favorites.

ARROYO GRANDE

WESTERN

Slickfork Custom Boots
558 Printz Road
(805) 481-4944
www.slickfork.com

Brent McCaslin operates a one-man show at this Arroyo Grande boot-making shop. Only offering custom-made boots, from work boots to lace-ups, traditional and more funky cowboy styles, and kangaroo to buffalo skins, Slickfork works on an individual basis to make unique footwear just right for you.

BURBANK

WESTERN

Baron California Hats
1619 West Burbank Boulevard
(818) 563-3025
www.baronhats.com

If you want to play Zorro, Indiana Jones, or even the Lone Ranger, just order up a custom hat from this supplier to the big Hollywood studios. The team of milliners can make just about any hat-related dream a reality, so let your imagination run wild.

DESCANSO

WESTERN

Woodward Custom Boots
(619) 659-5040
www.woodwardboots.com

Choose from a variety of hides—alligator, ostrich, stingray, or cow—for your custom-made cowboy boots crafted by John Woodward. The lines, colors, and designs are traditional and beautiful, and the hides can be dyed any color of the rainbow to suit your own taste. Call at least a day in advance to book an appointment and get directions to the studio.

FULLERTON

WESTERN

Gary's Belt Buckles
1272 Valle Vista Drive
(714) 526-6122
(800) 672-3353
www.garyscustomsaddleryandsilver.com

Custom-made silver overlay belt buckles are the specialty of this shop near Los Angeles, which brings traditional Western belt buckle designs into the twentieth century. From rodeo trophy buckles to others customized with your name, initials, or company logo, no job is too difficult for these expert metal-smiths. Prices start at around $100 per buckle.

LAGUNA BEACH

NATIVE AMERICAN

Len Wood's Indian Territory
305 North Coast Highway, #D
(949) 497-5747
www.indianterritory.com

This large gallery features an ample assortment of antique and contemporary Native American crafts. The back room houses a museum of sorts; it is a space spilling over with baskets, textiles, pottery, and other interesting specimens from Native American tribes of the Southwest.

LONG BEACH

HISPANIC

*American Museum of Straw Art
2324 Snowden Avenue
(562) 431-3540
www.strawartmuseum.org

This astonishing collection chronicles the history and art of straw in a series of fascinating exhibitions. Among the mind-boggling objects made of straw from around the world are several fine examples of New Mexican crosses using the straw appliqué technique.

LOS ANGELES

Though Los Angeles is usually equated with the new-fangled rather than the old-fashioned, a few pockets of traditional craftsmanship endure.

GENERAL CRAFTS

Autry National Center, Museum Stores
4700 Western Heritage Way
(323) 667-2000
www.autrynationalcenter.org

The Autry National Center unites the Southwest Museum of the American Indian and the Museum of the American West in one of the nation's premier research collections on Western culture. In addition to a worthwhile permanent collection, check the changing calendar for exhibitions that touch all three cultures of the Southwest. The museum stores carry a fine selection of traditional and contemporary crafts from Native American, Anglo, and Hispanic cultures.

Los Angeles Craft and Folk Art Museum, Museum Shop
5814 Wilshire Boulevard
(323) 937-4230

This little-known museum displays examples of craftsmanship from around the world. Sift through the global goodies in the first-floor gift shop to pick up some nice examples of Hispanic and local Western handmade goods.

WESTERN

Falconhead Boots, Belts, and Buckles
11911 San Vincente Boulevard, Suite 150
(310) 471-7075

In the Brentwood section of town, even die-hard city slickers can outfit themselves in handmade cowboy hats, boots, belts, buckles, and other Western wear. Falconhead takes custom orders on each item and also offers a small selection of Native American jewelry to top off your outfit. Expect to pay top dollar for custom-outfitted Western wear in the heart of L.A.

OLYMPIC VALLEY

NATIVE AMERICAN

Squaw Valley Trading Post
1600 Squaw Valley Road
(530) 583-6468

This rug-selling institution near Lake Tahoe offers some two thousand Zapotec weavings, which hang from the ceiling and are stacked on every available surface in the store. A small selection of pueblo pottery and turquoise jewelry rounds out the inventory.

SAN DIEGO

HISPANIC

*Artes de México
Shops at Bazaar del Mundo
Old Town San Diego State Historic Park
4133 Taylor Street
(619) 296-3161

In the inner depths of the Bazaar del Mundo, this store houses the city's best selection of authentic, fine-quality Mexican crafts, from Day of the Dead ceramic figures to crosses and milagros, Talavera pottery, tinware, retablos, bultos, and other goods. Prices are competitive; crosses with milagros, for example, run $40 to $100.

El Centro Artesano
Old Town San Diego State Historic Park
2637 San Diego Avenue
(619) 297-2931

The name is misleading; this is neither an artisan shop, nor a center. A tall wrought iron fence surrounds an enormous courtyard spilling over with wind chimes and garden pottery. The best bet for handcrafted goods is in the colorful Talavera pottery that lines the courtyard, but you have to poke around the more commercially produced goods for a few nice handcrafted pieces.

The Guatemala Shop
Shops at Bazaar del Mundo
Old Town San Diego State Historic Park
2754 Calhoun Street
(619) 296-3161

A nice selection of handwoven rugs, santos, and other goods from Guatemala, Mexico, and other Latin American craft centers fill every nook and cranny of this shop in the arcade of the Bazaar del Mundo.

Mex-Art Inc.
1155 Morena Boulevard
(619) 276-5810
www.mexartpottery.com

If you are seeking a lovely handcrafted pot for your garden, this is a great source. Mex-Art carries outdoor pottery from central Mexico, all handmade of terra-cotta. Be careful not to leave these pots outside in freezing temperatures, as the cold can cause them to crack or crumble.

*Tinsmith
Old Town San Diego State Historic Park
2613 San Diego Avenue
(619) 297-2616

Watch metalsmiths crafting wonderful pieces of tin in the back of this Old Town shop. I bought a lovely star Christmas ornament with a hinged piece for just $8, and many more bargains abound on frames, luminaries, candlesticks, ornaments, and large-scale angels.

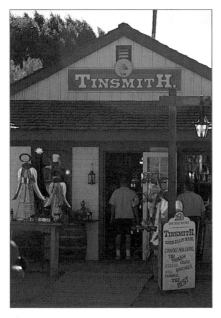

NATIVE AMERICAN

Angel's Indian Jewelry
Old Town San Diego State Historic Park
2424 San Diego Avenue
(619) 295-8801

Although the Apache Trading Post across the street is larger and better known, Angel's boasts better quality overall. The small but fine collection of Navajo and Apache jewelry is the best offering in the shop.

*Four Winds Trading
Old Town San Diego State Historic Park
2448-B San Diego Avenue
(619) 692-0466
(888) 545-5537

2476B San Diego Avenue
(619) 683-3214

Four Winds Trading runs the best Native American shops in San Diego, with an ample

selection of jewelry, katsinam, weavings, baskets, and other goods. They have two locations in Old Town and host a "Meet the Artist" series on a regular basis.

WESTERN

Toler's Leather Depot
Old Town San Diego State Historic Park
2625 Calhoun Street
(619) 295-7511
www.tolersleather.com

When you enter Toler's Leather Depot, the floor creaks beneath your feet and a pleasant leather aroma wafts through the air of this building from another era. Belts, hats, small leather gifts, and hand-tooled purses in the $100 range round out a small but nice selection of handmade leather goods.

Trails West Silver & Leather Company
821 West Harbor Drive
(619) 232-0553

Among the clothing and commercial goods for sale in this seaport-area shop are a few handcrafted pieces of jewelry and leather that make it worth a stop.

SANTA BARBARA

HISPANIC

Michael Haskell Antiques
539 San Ysidro Road
(805) 565-1121
www.michaelhaskell.com

A feast for the eyes, this gallery reflects the good taste and eye of its owner, who chooses only the highest-quality Spanish colonial furniture and decorative wares. In addition to rustic furniture and architectural pieces from the seventeenth and eighteenth centuries, the gallery carries reproduction lighting and other beautiful objects. It is located in Montecito, on the eastern outskirts of Santa Barbara.

TEHACHAPI

WESTERN

Robert Chavez Saddles
23869 Clover Springs Road
(661) 822-8802
www.rcsaddle.com

North of Los Angeles, saddle craftsman
Robert Chavez can realize your dream saddle
from quality leather and expert tooling. Finished pieces run from $3,000 to $4,000.

VENICE

GENERAL CRAFTS

*K. R. Martindale
1154 Grant Avenue
(310) 822-9145
www.americanindianartshow.com

K. R. Martindale has earned a reputation for
dealing in excellent quality Native American
and Hispanic crafts, both antique and contemporary, with lovely examples of Native
American baskets. The company also produces
several important art and antiques shows in
California.

NATIVE AMERICAN

*Zuni Pueblo
222 Main Street
(310) 399-7792

This Zuni tribal cooperative specializes in traditional Zuni fetishes as well as silver jewelry
set with turquoise, shell, and coral. Co-op
artisans can realize a custom piece.

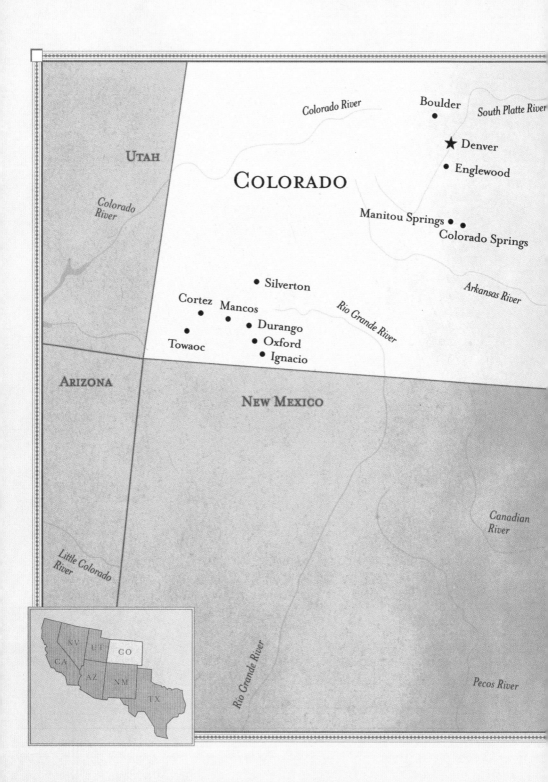

SOUTHWESTERN COLORADO

D istinct from the rest of the state in culture, history, and geography, southwestern Colorado boasts strong historical roots in all three craft traditions—Hispanic, Native American, and Western. The San Juan mountain range isolates this region from the rest of the state, home to Mesa Verde and the Four Corners—areas rich in Native American archeology.

As far back as 20,000 years ago nomadic hunters followed herds of woolly mammoth and bison across the mountainous landscape of what is now Colorado. But today's Native Americans of Colorado trace their lineage back to the Anasazi, the same ancient ancestors of Arizona and New Mexico's Pueblo people. From 1500 onward, the Arapahoe, Comanche, and the Ute also inhabited the region. Baskets and pottery dominated the craft traditions of the ancient Coloradans, as these vessels played a vital role in gathering, preparing, and serving food. The native populations of southwestern Colorado were cliff dwellers, like their New Mexican neighbors, and significant archeological remains stand in Mesa Verde National Park and Cortez.

Hispanic settlers moved into southwestern Colorado after they had already established stable communities in New Mexico. The Ute and Comanche resisted Hispanic colonization, though the region became an official colony of Spain in the eighteenth century. Certain Hispanic craft traditions, particularly religious works such as santos, left a strong impression. Today, some of the most significant museum and private collections of Hispanic works are in Colorado.

Rumors of gold lured Anglos to Colorado in the 1850s, and while it didn't live up to its promise, mining silver, copper, and other minerals remained an important industry until the turn of the twentieth century. In 1876 Colorado gained statehood, about the same time that its mining boom was in full swing.

The Old West still lives on in southwestern Colorado thanks to its cowboy culture. A specific type of spur developed here, incorporating influences of Texas and California—a testament to Colorado's role as a crossroads of the Southwest.

Listings preceded by an asterisk (*) denote my personal favorites.

BOULDER

NATIVE AMERICAN

Smith-Klein Gallery
1116 Pearl Street
(303) 444-7200
www.smithklein.com

Located in the pedestrian Pearl Street shopping district filled with commercial goods for tourists, Smith-Klein stands out for the quality of its works. More of a fine arts gallery, it is notable for the hundreds of antique and contemporary Zuni fetishes on display.

COLORADO SPRINGS

HISPANIC

*Taylor Museum
Colorado Springs Fine Arts Center
30 West Dale Street
(719) 634-5581
www.csfineartscenter.org

It may seem an unlikely place to find New Mexican santos, but the Taylor Museum collection is one of the country's best, holding more than seven hundred examples of this important colonial tradition.

NATIVE AMERICAN

Flute Player Gallery
2511 West Colorado Avenue
(719) 632-7702

Flute Player is a gallery-style space, with a collection of high-quality Native American goods ranging from Navajo jewelry to Zuni fetishes, weavings, and Hopi katsinam.

The Great Southwest
76 South Sierra Madre Street
(719) 471-7772

If you need an appraisal of your collection of Native American wares, Christopher Jones will happily oblige. While there, check out the nice selection of pueblo pottery, jewelry, fetishes, weavings, and katsinam.

WESTERN

Adobe Walls Antique Mall and Trading Post

2808 West Colorado Avenue
(719) 635-3994
www.adobe-walls.com

This is one of the area's most fascinating places to look for antiques, offering a surprising assortment of Old West collectibles. Explore the nooks, crannies, and outside yard for artisanal spurs and saddles, authentic wagon wheels, and weird but wonderful cactus skeletons.

CORTEZ

NATIVE AMERICAN

*Crow Canyon Archaeological Center

23390 Road K
(970) 565-8975
(800) 422-8975
www.crowcanyon.org

If you want to try your hand at making Indian pottery, sign up for a weeklong pottery course at the Crow Canyon Archaeological Center. This in-depth program shows would-be potters how to gather local clay, hand-coil pots, and decorate them with yucca brushes and local paints according to the classic Mesa Verde black-on-white style of pottery that evolved in the region in ancient times. The Anasazi Heritage Center provides many models of ancient pieces uncovered in excavations.

Notah Dineh Trading Company & Museum

345 West Main Street
(800) 444-2024
www.notahdineh.com

Cortez is known as a hub of Native American craft, and Notah Dineh is one of its most interesting places to shop. If you're in the market for a quality Navajo rug, Notah Dineh is a great place to start. In addition to classic Navajo styles and patterns such as "Ganado red" and Two Grey Hills, it carries rugs of the Navajo and other tribes. The shop claims to have the largest-known Two Grey Hills rug,

which is displayed in the "museum." Notah Dineh also carries katsina dolls, beadwork, and other Native American crafts.

WESTERN

Nu-Way Western Wear

33 East Main Street
(970) 565-7673
www.nuwaywesternwear.com

Nu-Way carries a large selection of quality manufactured cowboy boots by Justin, Nocona, and others, as well as endless racks of clothing guaranteed to make you look smooth in the saddle. Check out the ladies' hand-crafted purses and belt buckles that can be custom engraved.

DENVER

HISPANIC

Denver Art Museum

100 West Fourteenth Avenue Parkway
(720) 865-5000
www.denverartmuseum.org

The Denver Art Museum houses a small but impressive collection of historical santos made by artisans of Colorado and New Mexico.

Old Santa Fe Pottery

2485 South Santa Fe Drive
(303) 871-9434

Don't get lost in this twenty-room megastore of Hispanic wares. Old Santa Fe carries everything from rustic furniture to wrought iron decorative items, pottery, and other goodies to bring a little warmth of the Southwest to your home.

Regis University

Dayton Memorial Library
3333 Regis Boulevard
(303) 458-4110

This relatively unknown collection of the Jesuit Regis University is one of the largest groupings of New Mexican santos in America and should be on the list of any serious collector or aficionado who wants to learn more about these rustic works.

NATIVE AMERICAN

Mudhead Gallery
555 Seventeenth Street
(303) 293-0007
www.mudheadgallery.net

Located in the Hyatt Regency hotel, the Mudhead Gallery is a good choice for picking up pottery from San Ildefonso, Acoma, Santa Clara, and other New Mexico pueblos.

Native American Trading Company
1301 Bannock Street
(303) 534-0771
www.nativeamericantradingco.com

Located across from the Denver Art Museum, this pleasant store is a good bet for quality Navajo rugs, pueblo pottery, baskets, jewelry, and other unique items. Many pieces are antiques.

West Southwest Gallery
257 Fillmore Street
(303) 321-4139
www.westsouthwest.com

Former museum professionals run this premier gallery of Native American crafts, and their connoisseurship is evident in the hand-picked selection of baskets, Zuni fetishes, pueblo pottery, and jewelry. A few contemporary Hispanic religious works round out this interesting collection.

WESTERN

*Rockmount Ranch Wear
1626 Wazee Street
(303) 629-7777
(800) 7 ROCKMO
www.rockmount.com

The inventor of the Western shirt with snaps, Rockmount is credited with helping to popularize Western wear in the United States. Since opening its doors in 1946, this American institution has outfitted the likes of Elvis Presley and Bob Dylan. See for yourself what all the buzz is about at the store and museum at their main location on Wazee Street.

DURANGO

Durango is southwestern Colorado's major city. Its main street harkens back to the days when the railroad was a novelty and miners strolled the sidewalks, and the area around Durango is littered with the remains of old silver and copper mines.

GENERAL CRAFTS

Durango Silver
(Formerly Hartman's Mercantile)
17897 Highway 160
(970) 247-5589
www.durangosilver.com
www.hartmansmercantile.com

Walk through an amazing arch created with thousands of deer antlers, and enter Durango Silver, one of Durango's best bets for Native

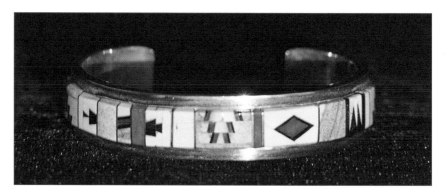

American jewelry and Western memorabilia. The display cases showcase antique and contemporary Navajo jewelry, mostly crafted with Bisbee Blue turquoise. Discover that unique antique among an enthralling collection of old spurs, saddles, Navajo rugs, and one-of-a-kind finds.

NATIVE AMERICAN

Hell Bent Leather & Silver
741 Main Avenue
(970) 247-9088
www.hellbentleather.com

Contemporary in spirit but inspired by the elaborate traditional beadwork of the Plains Indians, Hell Bent crafts lovely beaded purses and leather bags inspired by Native American designs of the past. The backpack-style bags with beaded ornamentation are a personal favorite.

Indian Village
17897 Highway 160
(970) 259-3100
www.indianvillage.com

Here is a chance to watch jewelry makers in action as they craft traditional bracelets, pendants, belt buckles, bolo ties, rings, and other pieces from silver and turquoise, mostly the coveted Bisbee Blue stone. Many of the works are created on-site, while others are made by Native American artisans off-site.

A Shared Blanket
736 Main Avenue
(970) 247-9210
www.asharedblanket.com

A Shared Blanket assembles an expert staff to help you get the most from the hand-selected Navajo rugs, pueblo pottery, baskets, Zuni fetishes, drums and flutes, and silver jewelry on display. In addition to a resident archeologist who can tell you more about the antique and contemporary works as you browse, the staff can coordinate custom orders from turquoise jewelry to hand-painted drums. Artisans are usually working on-site.

Toh-Atin Gallery
145 West Ninth Street
(970) 247-8277
www.toh-atin.com

The main attraction in this well-regarded establishment are the fine Navajo weavings that the gallery's founder, Jackson Clark, began trading in the 1950s. Today, in addition to all the major styles of Navajo rugs, you'll find pueblo pottery, silver and turquoise jewelry, and other unique Native American works.

IGNACIO

NATIVE AMERICAN

Southern Ute Museum, Gift Shop
1426 Highway 172
(970) 563-4649

For authentic crafts of Colorado's Native American Ute people, this museum store is a great choice. The shop carries a wide selection of jewelry, as well as beaded moccasins, weavings, and a few other wares from other southwestern tribes. The shop is endorsed by the Indian Arts and Crafts Board of the U.S. Department of the Interior, so you can buy with confidence. The museum is located one mile north of Ignacio along Highway 172.

WESTERN

Cowboys Toys
20750 Highway 151
(970) 884-9415
www.cowboys-toys.com

Everything a cowboy requires—from custom-made boots to hand tooled saddles, leather chaps, even handcrafted wooden display stands for your saddle that rock back and forth! In addition to the fine handmade cowboy wear and gear, look for handmade cowboy decorative items for the home from lamps to toilet-seat covers embellished with hand-tooled leather.

MANCOS

WESTERN

Bartel's Mancos Valley Stage Line
4550 County Road 41
(970) 533-9857
(800) 365-3530
www.thestagecoach.com

If you're a serious collector ready for a new frontier, $9,800 will buy you an authentic historical reproduction of an 1800s-era stagecoach or oil wagon. While you browse this unique collection of antiques, sign up to take a stagecoach tour of the local canyons with Western history enthusiast Eric Bartels.

Nathaniel's of Colorado
121 West Grand Avenue
(970) 533-9740
(866) 533-9740
www.nathanielsofcolorado.com

Quality custom headgear is the main attraction at this Mancos hattery, a favorite with Colorado politicians and celebrities. Choose from beaver or rabbit fur, and decide on a style that's right for you. All hats are handcrafted using antique equipment and old techniques. Finish it off with a custom-designed hatband or choose from a wide selection on-site. You'll wait about five weeks to get your hat, but rest assured it will fit your head better than any hat you've ever worn.

Prices range from $250 to $600. The proprietor, Nathaniel Funmaker, may be the only Native American master hatter in the country.

MANITOU SPRINGS

NATIVE AMERICAN

Garden of the Gods Trading Post
324 Beckers Lane
(719) 685-9045
www.co-trading-post.com

This is the state's largest historic trading post, dating back to the 1920s. Although the trading post carries a lot of cheap souvenirs, the gallery also offers quality handcrafted Navajo rugs, jewelry, pueblo pottery, and other Native American crafts. Originally the building was designed to resemble Pueblo Indian dwellings, and its unique architecture, combined with buffalo burgers in the cafe, offer a one-of-a-kind Colorado experience. It is located near the entrance to the Garden of the Gods Park.

SILVERTON

NATIVE AMERICAN

Ellis Tanner Gallery
1250 Greene Street
(970) 387-5785

Ellis Tanner of Gallup, New Mexico, fame operates this fourth-generation retail establishment. The best offering here is jewelry, such as chunky bracelets, rings, and pendants set with turquoise and coral.

Iron Horse Indian Store
1171 Greene Street
(970) 387-5808

Old Town Indian Shop
1219 Greene Street
(970) 387-5426

Ortega's Indian Trading Post
1228 Greene Street
(970) 387-5744

Sprawling along Greene Street in the center of Silverton, Debbie Ortega Noel runs the Iron Horse, the Old Town Indian Shop, and Ortega's Indian Trading Post. Look for pueblo pottery, quality handcrafted jewelry, and Zuni fetishes in all three stores.

TOWAOC

NATIVE AMERICAN

Ute Mountain Indian Pottery
Highway 160 South
(800) 896-8548

This tribe-owned pottery studio is a great place to watch Native American potters crafting the characteristic wares of the Ute, with black, red, and sometimes colorful geometric decoration. Pick up canteens, wedding vases, seed pots, and other wares for fair prices. The establishment is located about eight miles south of Cortez.

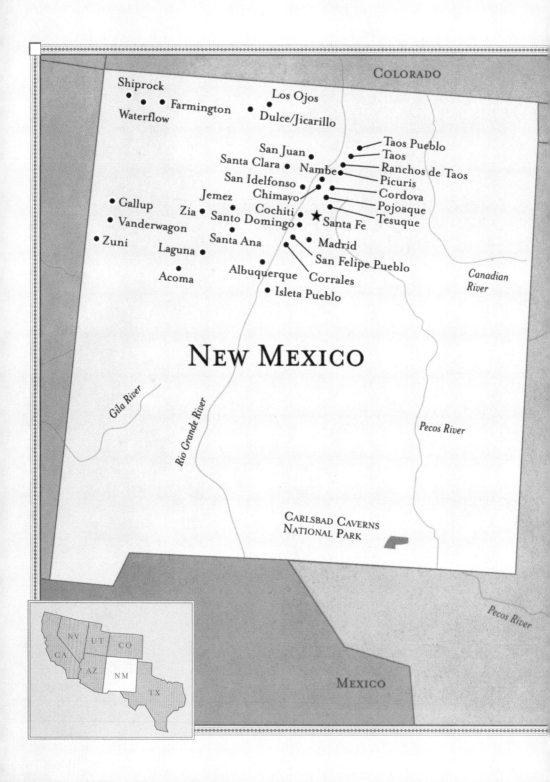

COLORADO

Shiprock
● ● ● Farmington
Waterflow

Los Ojos
●
Dulce/Jicarillo

San Juan ●
Santa Clara ● Nambe ●
San Idelfonso ●
Jemez ● Chimayo ●
Zia ● Cochiti
Gallup ● Santo Domingo ●
Vanderwagon ●
Zuni ●
Santa Ana ●
Laguna ●
Acoma ●
Albuquerque ●
Isleta Pueblo ●

Taos Pueblo
Taos
Ranchos de Taos
Picuris
Cordova
Pojoaque
Tesuque
★ Santa Fe

Madrid
San Felipe Pueblo
Corrales

Canadian
River

NEW MEXICO

Gila River

Rio Grande River

Pecos River

CARLSBAD CAVERNS
NATIONAL PARK

Pecos River

MEXICO

NV UT CO
CA
AZ NM
TX

NEW MEXICO

New Mexico is a patchwork quilt of culture and history that spans some twenty-five millennia. The state is one of the richest repositories of Native American, Hispanic, and Western cultural patrimony, and every town boasts important craftspeople following in the footsteps of their ancestors.

Human habitation in New Mexico can be traced as far back as 25,000 BC, making it one of the most ancient lands in the nation. The cliff-dwelling Anasazi and the Mogollon established stable, agriculturally based villages as early as 3000 BC. Ancient pottery remains attest that this craft was already sophisticated. Seashells and feathers of non-native birds prove that they were experienced traders with some knowledge of a world beyond their own lands. The Pueblo peoples who populate New Mexico's Native American communities today descended from the ancient Anasazi. The Pueblo people inherited from their ancestors a knowledge of monumental architecture, highly developed pottery, village life, and agriculture.

Spanish explorers traveled north along the Rio Grande in the mid-sixteenth century in search of the mythical "seven cities of gold" that they imagined must exist based on their experience discovering the fabulous Aztec ruins in Mexico. Of course, they found Pueblo Indians minding their own business and living in adobe dwellings instead. However, the political influence of the Spanish endured in what was a province of New Spain for the next three hundred years; its capital was in Santa Fe. Nowhere in America was the influence of the Spanish more deeply ingrained as in New Mexico, and the cultural influence of this Hispanic past can be felt throughout New Mexico today. Catholic missions sprang up in the pueblos during the seventeenth century, and there was a vibrant interchange of craft production between the Hispanic and native cultures. Periods of violence also characterized their interchange, most notably during the 1680 pueblo revolt against the Spanish that brought together tribes that had never before been united. Nevertheless, Hispanic areas were resettled and firmly reestablished by the time the first Anglos set foot in the territory.

Anglos arrived around the turn of the nineteenth century, at first on trading missions. Renegade "mountain men" headed into the mountains above Taos to trap beaver and other game for their furs, and many married into Hispanic and Native American families. By the end of the Mexican-American War in 1848, New Mexico was firmly within the grasp of the new Americans.

Listings preceded by an asterisk (*) denote my personal favorites.

ACOMA PUEBLO

If you're choosing a quality souvenir of the Native American Southwest, you can't do much better than a pot from Acoma, one of New Mexico's premier centers of traditional pueblo pottery. Acoma wares are famous for their stark black-and-white geometric patterns that sometimes create an optical illusion. You can buy confidently from individual potters hawking their wares from their homes or outdoor stalls at the bottom and top of the mesa, as well as the pueblo's main Sky City Cultural Center.

Pueblo Pottery Gallery
(800) 933-5771
www.pueblopotterygallery.com

Located in the center of Acoma pueblo, this is a good choice for quality Acoma seed pots, wedding vases, and other vessels, as well as katsinam and other miscellaneous crafts.

*Sky City Cultural Center
(800) 747-0181

If you prefer to buy from a traditional store rather than directly from the artisan, this is a great choice for authentic Acoma pottery. Take in the fabulous views from atop the Sky City mesa while browsing for the perfect pot.

ALBUQUERQUE

For value and selection of handmade crafts—Hispanic, Native American, and Western—there is no better place than Old Town Albuquerque. The variety of goods within a few city blocks makes it my pick for the best shopping experience in the Southwest.

GENERAL CRAFTS

Angel Town
419-B San Felipe Street NW
(505) 243-8490
(888) 334-0589
www.angeltownnm.com

This likable shop specializes in angels from around the world, including some Native American examples crafted from fabric and ceramic that I haven't seen anywhere else. It's especially worth a stop, though, to see the work of the New Mexico–based Alvarez family of carvers. They craft beautiful, rustic angels from rough-hewn limbs and cottonwood roots. No two are alike, and their sizes range from as small as Christmas ornaments up to several feet tall.

Cowboys & Indians Antiques
4000 Central Avenue SE
(505) 255-4054
www.cowboysandindiansnm.com

The fantastic hodgepodge at this shop is one of the Southwest's best collections of gently used Native American crafts and Western memorabilia, with a smattering of Hispanic devotional art thrown in. On any given day you might uncover dusty hand-tooled saddles, antique katsina dolls, rusty spurs, vintage cowboy prints, historic signs, a Mexican sombrero, pueblo pottery, a worn bulto, squash blossom necklaces, Navajo rugs, Zuni fetishes, and more one-of-a-kind treasures. The owner, Terry Schurmeier, organizes the popular Great Southwestern Antiques, Indian & Old West Show that takes place in Albuquerque each summer (see the Calendar of Southwestern Craft Festivals and Events). Cowboys & Indians is located on historic Route 66 in the artsy Nob Hill district of Albuquerque.

Hanging Tree Gallery
416 Romero Street NW
(505) 842-1420

Mostly a gallery of paintings, Hanging Tree also carries an eclectic selection of antique and contemporary silver jewelry, Navajo weavings, pueblo pottery from Santa Clara and San Ildefonso, and a few additional items such as baskets, concha belts, and bolos. It also has some antique Western wear, including boots, saddles, gun leather, spurs, and horse tack.

Pimentel Guitars
3316 Lafayette Drive NE
(505) 884-1669
www.pimentelguitars.com

My friend and fellow guitar enthusiast John Alcorn led me to this family of excellent guitar craftsmen. Order a custom-made instrument with your choice of mahogany, maple, walnut, or another wood for the back and sides, as well as custom-decorated rosettes and fingerboards.

HISPANIC

Albuquerque Museum of Art and History Museum Shop
2000 Mountain Road NW
(505) 242-4600
www.cabq.gov/museum

With one of the largest permanent collections of Spanish colonial objects in the country, the Albuquerque Museum is a great place to start your foray into the Hispanic craft traditions of New Mexico. The weaving demonstration is particularly well done. La Tienda museum shop carries a small selection of quality hand-crafted jewelry, pottery, and textiles. The museum is located one block east of the Plaza.

Casa Talamantes
2424 Candelaria Road NE
(505) 265-2977
www.casatalamantes.com

Although the inventory is virtually all crafted in Mexico, this shop offers a nice selection of Spanish colonial–style furniture, Talavera pottery and tile, tinware, Day of the Dead crafts, jewelry, santos, and other Hispanic devotional arts. Casa Talamantes also carries an attractive array of handmade classical, Flamenco, and Mariachi guitars.

*Hispaniae
410 Romero Street NW
(505) 244-1533
www.hispaniae.com

A relative newcomer to the Old Town shopping scene, Hispaniae is one of the best places to shop for Hispanic crafts in the Southwest. Hispaniae has a colorful selection of Talavera pottery, santos of all types, tinware, and other handmade goods in the Hispanic tradition. Particularly nice is the selection of crosses made of materials ranging from wood to pewter, and decorated with everything imaginable from metal milagros to bottle caps. An extensive Day of the Dead selection includes some delightful nichos, or niches displaying skeletons engaged in a variety of happy after-life activities.

National Hispanic Cultural Center of New Mexico, Gift Shop
1701 Fourth Street SW
(505) 246-2261
(877) 531-4107
www.nhccnm.org

An exciting new institution fostered by New Mexico's Department of Cultural Affairs, this museum celebrates the culture of Hispanics in New Mexico and throughout the world. It has a small gift shop appropriately called La Tiendita, which carries a few handmade wares from New Mexico and other countries.

Qué Chula
1427 Carlisle Boulevard NE
(505) 255-0515

This small shop tucked into a commercial strip mall specializes in rustic, Mexican furniture hand-painted in bright colors. Funky twists on traditional forms—the Day of the Dead chairs and armoires are a personal favorite—characterize the select and whimsical inventory that make this shop a visual delight.

*Saints & Martyrs
404-A San Felipe Street NW
(505) 224-9323
www.saints-martyrs.com

This is one of my favorite places to shop for crafts in the entire Southwest. Appropriately located alongside Our Lady of Guadalupe Chapel, Saints & Martyrs offers one of the region's most eclectic and high-quality collections of Hispanic religious crafts. Each piece is unique; many are antiques. The selection changes constantly: you might find a saint's leg from a church in Mexico, a retablo featuring St. Francis, an antique Virgin Mary with real clothes, crosses decorated with glass, unique rosaries, and wonderful lacework. This is one of only a handful of places where you can usually find high-quality objects made with straw inlay or appliqué. For museum quality at a fair price, this is one of the region's best dealers.

Santos Traditional & Religious Art ¡Traditions! A Festival Marketplace
601 West Frontage Road, #690
(505) 771-0800
www.santosnm.com

This shop offers a nice selection of Hispanic religious crafts, including full-fledged altarpieces and crosses, as well as every incarnation of santos and other Hispanic religious art. The store is located inside ¡Traditions! A Festival Marketplace, which bills itself as a mall of traditional crafts at reasonable prices. It sounds more tantalizing than it actually is, but Santos makes it worth a stop. ¡Traditions! is located between Albuquerque and Santa Fe at Exit 257 off of I-25.

NATIVE AMERICAN

Agape Southwest Pueblo Pottery
414 Romero Road NW
(505) 243-2366
www.agapesw.com

Agape offers a wide selection of the major pottery styles from the nineteen pueblos of New Mexico, ranging in price from several hundred to several thousand dollars. In addition to a small selection of weavings and katsinam, displays showcase unique pieces of Native American jewelry.

Bear Paw Indian Arts and Gallery
328 San Felipe Street NW
(505) 843-9337

Endorsed by the Indian Arts and Crafts Board, Bear Paw carries a variety of authentic Native American wares from Navajo weavings to katsina dolls, drums and flutes, jewelry, and pueblo pottery.

*Bien Mur Indian Market Center
100 Bien Mur Drive NE
(505) 821-5400
(800) 365-5400
www.bienmur.com

This place bills itself as the largest tribe-owned and tribe-operated Native American crafts store in the Southwest, and I believe it. In its unique two-story rotunda, the Bien Mur Indian Market Center houses what is certainly Albuquerque's widest selection of authentic Native American pottery, rugs, baskets, jewelry, katsina dolls, and other crafts. It carries an enormous supply of crafts from all the New Mexico pueblos, as well as a good selection of Hopi and Navajo wares. Prices are generally lower than on the Navajo and Hopi reservations, making Bien Mur a good value for guaranteed authenticity. Bien Mur is located on the reservation of Sandia Pueblo, on the northern outskirts of the city, which became a Spanish settlement in 1617. Bien Mur is endorsed by the Council for Indigenous Arts and Culture and the Indian Arts and Crafts Board.

Grandfather Eagle
202-A San Felipe Street NW
(505) 242-5376
www.grandfathereagle.com

A stunning Indian chief's headdress with feathers that dripped to the floor (including a $2,700 price tag) greeted me the first time I walked into this shop. But the real specialty here is handmade Native American jewelry, including uniquely southwestern pieces such as bolo ties and belt buckles. The shop specializes in one-of-a-kind jewelry incorporating creamy white elk ivory.

House of the Shalako
20 First Plaza Galeria, #65
(505) 242-4579
www.houseoftheshalako.com

In spite of its off-the-beaten-track location near the Albuquerque Convention Center, House of the Shalako has built a loyal clientele of repeat customers over the past three decades. Its reputation is due to its inventory—high-quality katsinam, pottery, Navajo weavings, and other miscellaneous pieces. House of the Shalako is a member of the Indian Arts and Crafts Association, which upholds the industry's standards of authenticity and fair practices for Native American craftspeople.

Indian Pueblo Cultural Center, Gift Shop
2401 Twelfth Street NW
(505) 843-7270
www.indianpueblo.org

This admirable nonprofit institution assembles works from the nineteen pueblos of New Mexico. The gift shop offers a fine selection of high-quality pottery, jewelry, textiles, and other Native American works, and you can rest assured that you are buying authentic Native American crafts. On the weekends, catch the demonstrations of Native American weavers, jewelry makers, potters, and other artisans.

Museum of Turquoise, Museum Shop
2107 Central Avenue NW
(505) 247-8650

Enter this unique museum through a reconstructed turquoise mine tunnel, and discover the history of mining the blue stone that has been precious to Native American jewelry artisans for centuries. Exhibits display stones from more than sixty mines around the world. The museum shop hosts demonstrations of turquoise cutting and polishing, and it features Native American silversmiths on a regular basis. The shop also carries some quality pieces of jewelry incorporating every shade of turquoise from white to green and bright and muted blue.

New Mexico Bead and Fetish
401 Romero Street NW
(505) 243-2600
(800) 687-2701
www.nmbeadandfetish.com

Unleash your creativity at this Old Town shop, whose showroom consists of trays upon trays of beads. Some of the beads are handcrafted by Native Americans from turquoise, shell, and horn. Authentic Zuni fetishes can even be strung on a necklace or bracelet; a special display case exhibits the more traditional Zuni fetish figurines.

Penfield Gallery of Indian Arts
2043 South Plaza Street NW
(505) 242-9696
www.penfieldgallery.com

A favorite among locals, the Penfield Gallery stuffs a wide selection of Native American crafts—pottery, jewelry, Navajo weavings, katsinam, baskets, and more—into a small Old Town space. Penfield family members have been dealers of Indian art for nearly a century. Today, they are known for offering one of Old Town's widest selections of Zuni fetishes.

*Santo Domingo Indian Trading Post
401 San Felipe Street NW
(505) 764-0129

One of the few Indian-owned and Indian-operated stores in Old Town Albuquerque, Santo Domingo Indian Trading Post specializes in jewelry from Santo Domingo Pueblo and a few other reservations. In a no-frills atmosphere, you can usually watch artisans crafting pieces on-site and chat with the friendly staff happy to provide details about their work. Most of the pieces are a good value.

Silver Sun
2011 Central Avenue NW
(505) 246-9692
(800) 662-3220
www.silversunalbuquerque.com

A well-regarded Indian jewelry shop with owners on the board of the Indian Arts and Crafts Association, Silver Sun employs Native American artisans on staff. The store carries a fine selection of mostly Navajo traditional turquoise jewelry crafted of the many shades from Southwest mines both depleted and still in operation.

Warpath Trading Post
303 Romero Street NW, #204
(505) 243-6993

The pure volume of silver jewelry filling the glass display cases of the Warpath Trading Post will boggle the mind of even veteran Indian jewelry shoppers. If you're seeking a particular traditional design, chances are you'll find it here. Warpath also carries some additional authentic Native American crafts, including katsinam and Zuni fetishes.

Wright's Indian Art
The Courtyard, Lower Level
San Mateo and Lomas boulevards
(505) 266-0120
www.wrightsgallery.com

The almost-hidden location of this shop—tucked under and behind a row of street-facing storefronts on a busy commercial strip—bears witness to a loyal following of clients. In contrast to many Native American craft dealers who load every square inch of their shops to the brim, Wright's carefully selects only the highest-quality pieces and lovingly curates them in glass cases and other displays around the shop. The result is an eclectic and quality representation of New Mexican pueblo craft.

WESTERN

Ghost Town Trading Co.
111 Carlisle Boulevard NE
(505) 255-5656
(888) 224-8280
www.ghosttowntrading.com

Take some weathered planks of ponderosa pine, assemble them, add a few pieces of antique hardware, and voilà—you've got a one-of-a-kind piece of Western decor. That's exactly what Ghost Town Trading offers its clients—custom furniture and accessories in the rustic spirit of the Southwest. It also carries a line of unique, rough-hewn pieces made of antique cedar, fir, pine, and redwood, which are embellished creatively with pieces of leather, moldings, tinware, and wrought iron. The store is located in the Nob Hill section of town.

Vigil's Saddle Shop
8008 Rio Grande Boulevard NW
(505) 898-1489

Ricardo Vigil has earned a reputation for crafting quality handmade saddles and silver accessories from his modest shop in Albuquerque.

CHIMAYÓ

Chimayó is a must-see village for craft and history buffs. A center of weaving for centuries, Chimayó is also home to an important sanctuary and historic Spanish colonial church. Best of all, the quiet setting is perfect for wandering around the church grounds and weaving studios.

HISPANIC

Casa Feliz Gallery
Highway 98
(505) 351-2470

Casa Feliz is worth a stop to tour the historic adobe hacienda that houses an impressive selection of Chimayó rugs and handwoven vests and jackets, as well as Native American jewelry, pottery, and katsinam. You can custom order apparel woven in traditional Chimayó patterns. The owners are passionate about their inventory and their historic

family home, and will generously share their knowledge and passion for Chimayó.

Centinela Traditional Arts
Centinela Ranch
(505) 351-2180
www.chimayoweavers.com

The members of the Trujillo family are some of the premier weavers in the country, and for the Chimayó, this family is one of the most important forces in passing the torch of this tradition into the future. Stop in to watch weavers at their looms, and browse the impressive tapestry gallery that displays all of the major historic weaving styles of the Rio Grande area. In addition to rugs and wall hangings, you can pick up vests and jackets woven in the traditional styles.

Chimayó Trading & Mercantile
Highway 76
(505) 351-4566
(800) 248-7859
www.chimayoarts.com

Chimayó Trading offers a wide selection of typical rugs, as well as carvings, baskets, Native American katsinam, and pottery.

CORDOVA

HISPANIC

Castillo Gallery
On the High Road to Taos
(505) 351-4067
www.castillogallery.com

The picturesque village of Cordova has been famous for years for its small community of wood-carvers who craft rustic santos of juniper and aspen. The Castillo Gallery is located on the main road in Cordova and specializes in the restrained and beautiful style of New Mexico's traditional wood-carvers.

CORRALES

HISPANIC

Casa San Ysidro
(505) 898-3915

This stunning private collection, recently turned into a branch of the Albuquerque Museum, re-creates what life was like in Spanish colonial New Mexico, complete with santos, furniture, and weavings artfully displayed in a very special home. Corrales is located just north of Albuquerque on the road to Santa Fe.

DULCE

Dulce is the tribal headquarters of the Jicarilla Apache. Jicarilla translates loosely as "basket," a reference to the craft for which this group is famous. The Jicarilla are also known for their fabulous beadwork, which decorates leather bags, moccasins, and ceremonial apparel.

NATIVE AMERICAN

Jicarilla Arts and Crafts Museum, Museum Shop
10 Jicarilla Boulevard, Highway 64
(505) 759-4274

Locally made baskets and beadwork are offered for sale in the museum shop, and you can rest assured that you're buying quality, authentic works.

FARMINGTON

NATIVE AMERICAN

Foutz Indian Room
301 West Main Street
(505) 325-9413

The Foutz family has operated the Teec Nos Pos Trading Post in Arizona for four generations, specializing in the Teec Nos Pos style of Navajo weavings. The Farmington location carries a variety of Native American crafts, and supplies Indian weavers with wool to practice their craft.

Navajo Trading Company
126 East Main Street
(505) 325-1685

This shop is worth a stop if you are a fan of Indian pawn, antique jewelry exchanged by Native Americans for more practical goods. Prices can be steep for large or unique pieces, or those that incorporate sizeable stones. Even if you don't buy, you can try out your Navajo language skills with the helpful staff.

GALLUP

Gallup is a major center for Native American crafts, thanks to its location between the Navajo reservation and the pueblos of western New Mexico. The town bustles with trading posts and pawn shops serving the nearby Indian communities and doing business with artisans who supply the stores. Because of this proximity to the source as well as healthy competition among local dealers, you can pick up some good values on turquoise and silver jewelry, concha belts, textiles, beadwork, and katsina dolls. Gallup also has some tourist traps and a few places selling wares that are not Indian-made. Watch out for heavily discounted crafts; if the prices seem too good to be true, chances are the crafts are not authentic.

NATIVE AMERICAN

*Ellis Tanner Trading Company
Nizhoni Boulevard, at Highway 602
(505) 863-4434

On a windswept hilltop overlooking the Navajo Nation, Ellis Tanner Trading Company offers everything from turquoise bracelets to horse feed, saddles, breakfast cereal, gasoline, check cashing, and even tax advice. Ellis Tanner represents the fourth generation of this family business, and he upholds the traditional role of the trading post as a one-stop shop for everything from turquoise jewelry to cookware and blankets. His pawn room holds more than forty thousand pieces, many of which Tanner says are reclaimed by their original owners at some point. Ellis Tanner Trading Company is endorsed by the Council for Indigenous Arts and Culture as one of the Southwest's premier places to buy authentic Native American crafts.

Gilbert Ortega's
3306 East Highway 66
(505) 722-6666
www.gilbertortegas.com

Gilbert Ortega's is worth a stop just to gawk at what is billed as the largest chunk of turquoise in the world. Its owners estimate the nugget's value at just under $200,000. While there, browse a fine selection of handmade goods from all the major tribes of the Southwest. The inventory of jewelry and textiles is especially strong.

M & M Trading
1218 East Highway 66
(505) 863-4995
www.newmexicocarvings.com

If you're in the market for Zuni fetishes, M & M is a good bet. My favorite are the tiny animals strung on long necklaces, but the artisans here also craft more unusual pieces like bolo ties and earrings with fetish animals.

*Navajo Spirit Southwestern Wear
815 West Coal Avenue
(505) 722-6837
www.navajospirit.com

Here is a unique souvenir of the Southwest that you can wear with pride: handmade clothing in Western and Navajo styles, designed by Virginia Yazzie-Ballenger. From Western-style shirts to flowing tiered skirts, all of the designs are high quality and handcrafted.

Perry Null / Tobe Turpen Trading Co.
1710 South Second Street
(505) 863-5249
www.pntrader.com

In business for nearly a century and endorsed by the Council for Indigenous Arts and Culture, Perry Null specializes in Navajo, Hopi, and Zuni jewelry, including buckles, bolos, pins, earrings, bracelets, and pendants. The store also carries a variety of Zuni fetishes and features some fine examples of Native American weaving in its rug room.

Rain Bird Pawn & Trading Co.
1724 South Second Street
(505) 722-3292
www.rainbirdtrading.com

This third-generation trading family offers a wide selection of turquoise jewelry, antique pawned works, Navajo rugs, and other goodies in the expansive showroom next door to the lumber supply company the family also owns.

Richardson's Trading Company
222 West Historic Route 66
(505) 722-4762
www.richardsontrading.com

This old-fashioned trading post carries a good selection of Navajo and Zuni jewelry, from squash blossom necklaces to turquoise inlay bracelets, bolo ties, and concha belts.

Shush Yaz Trading Company
1304 West Lincoln Avenue
(505) 722-0130

This is the Gallup location of the Santa Fe family business that traces its history of trading with the Native Americans back some 120 years (see page 157). The Gallup store is located across from McDonald's on Route 66.

Thunderbird Supply
1907 West Historic Route 66
(505) 722-4323
www.thunderbirdsupply.com

Endorsed by the Council for Indigenous Arts and Culture, Thunderbird Supply has been providing Native American jewelry artisans with the basic materials of their craft for more than thirty years. Whether you're looking for beads made of turquoise, coral, or bone, or sheet metals for crafting jewelry, this is one of the Four Corners's premier sources for raw jewelry materials.

A Touch of Santa Fe
814 South Second Street
(505) 722-6999
www.atouchofsantafe.com

A relative newcomer to Gallup, A Touch of Santa Fe specializes in authentic Native American jewelry. Many of the pieces contain inlaid stones and are contemporary in spirit.

Trailblazer
212 South Second Street
(505) 722-5051
www.trailblaz.com

Chances are good that you can watch Native American artisans doing business with Trailblazer staff in this busy store. In addition to offering some quality Navajo jewelry and a few other miscellaneous crafts, Trailblazer also specializes in jewelry repair.

ISLETA PUEBLO

The Tiwa-speaking peoples of Isleta Pueblo are known for their distinctive red-and-black designs on white pottery, which you can purchase directly from artisans who hang "Open" signs on their doors or in their windows or at the Isleta Casino Resort Gift Shop. Isleta is located fourteen miles south of Albuquerque.

JEMEZ PUEBLO

Jemez is known for its distinctive pottery, but the pueblo is closed to visitors except for special feast days. You can always purchase from the Walatowa Visitor Center, or better yet, from a reputable dealer in nearby Santa Fe or Albuquerque.

Walatowa Visitor Center
7413 Highway 4
(505) 834-7235
www.jemezpueblo.org

A small gift shop at the visitor center offers Jemez pottery from numerous artisans of the pueblo.

LAGUNA

The Laguna people occupy six villages west of Albuquerque. Crafts are proudly displayed during feast days, or you can browse artisans' homes—look for "Open" signs in the windows or doors.

NATIVE AMERICAN

Dancing Eagle Casino and Travel Center
Exit 108 off of I-40
(505) 552-7777
(877) 440-9966
www.dancingeaglecasino.com

A small gift shop sells pottery and some other crafts made by Laguna artisans.

LOS OJOS

GENERAL CRAFTS

*Tierra Wools
91 Main Street
(505) 588-7231
(888) 709-0979
www.handweavers.com

If you are a fan of traditional weavings, Tierra Wools makes a detour to remote Los Ojos worthwhile. This enterprise is part of a nonprofit organization that raises and sheers sheep, washes the wool, spins it, then hand-weaves it into quality traditional rugs, blankets, pillows, apparel, and other goods. Tierra Wools is a major supplier of wool to artisans throughout New Mexico and the Southwest, and it is a great place to watch some of the region's most accomplished weavers at work at their looms. Staff people are knowledgeable and happy to share their passion for weaving with visitors.

MADRID

This was once an industrious mining town with an ample supply of coal and a now-depleted turquoise mine that is one of the oldest in the country. Today, Madrid counts three hundred residents and a thriving Bohemian artist community located along the Turquoise Trail that runs between Albuquerque and Santa Fe.

HISPANIC

Primitiva
2860 Main Street
(505) 471-7904
www.primitiva.com

Stumble out of the vintage Mine Shaft Tavern and down the street to Primitiva, where you'll find a bounty of Hispanic handmade goods and rustic furniture of alder wood. This is one of the largest retail spaces in Madrid, and every inch is filled with hand-selected Hispanic religious crafts and decorative items.

NATIVE AMERICAN

*Chumani Gallery
2839 State Highway 14
(505) 424-3813
www.chumanigallery.com

Todd Klippenstein is one of the more interesting personalities in a small town already chock-full of colorful characters. A Renaissance man and nationally known artist, Klippenstein has a hip selection of traditional and contemporary Native American jewelry. Klippenstein mines his own stones and incorporates them into custom-made jewelry, so you can dream up a design and make it a reality.

The Great Madrid Gift Emporium
2867 State Highway 14
(505) 471-7605
www.ghosttowntradingpost.com

This old cottage with creaking floors brims with silver and turquoise jewelry. There are a few pieces of average-quality Native American pottery and katsinam, but the real attraction is the nice selection of silver jewelry in both traditional and more contemporary styles. Although Madrid was once the center of an important turquoise mining industry, today most of the stones come from mines outside the U.S., including Mexico and Australia. The owners also operate a shop across the street with a similar inventory.

Seppanen & Daughters Fine Textiles
2879 State Road 14
(505) 424-7470
www.finetextiles.com

This rug shop, located in a converted cottage along Madrid's main drag, exudes warmth and comfort. Seppanen specializes in an eclectic mix of rugs from the Navajo nation, Tibet, and Oaxaca, Mexico, which are stacked and artfully arranged throughout the store alongside exotic Tibetan furniture. This is truly a handpicked and quality selection, and each piece is priced accordingly. Look for the front porch draped with colorful rugs.

NAMBÉ PUEBLO

Nambé is a peaceful oasis with stunning views of the Sangre de Cristo mountains and waterfalls on the grounds of the pueblo. Register at the pueblo entrance, then look for local homes with "Open" signs. Weaving, beadwork, and pottery are the major craft traditions here.

PICURIS PUEBLO

The best place to buy crafts in this small, remote pueblo is the Picuris Pueblo Museum; the museum shop carries nice examples of the tribe's signature glittery micaceous pottery, as well as beadwork, weaving, and pottery.

POJOAQUE PUEBLO

Poeh Cultural Center
(505) 455-3334
www.poehcenter.com

This nice shop sells the pueblo's crafts.

Pojoaque Pueblo Visitor Center
Highway 285 and 84
(505) 455-3460

This is a friendly place to buy crafts, with a nice selection of local pottery, rugs, and katsinam.

RANCHOS DE TAOS

GENERAL CRAFTS

Featherston Trading Company
#66 Ranchos Church Plaza
(505) 758-1252
www.featherstontrading.com

Featherston Trading specializes in both Native American and Western works, and carries an eclectic selection of unusual handmade leather bags, antique spurs, silver jewelry, Hopi katsi-

nam, and other one-of-a-kind treasures. If you're in the market for a decorative skull, it carries a wide selection of cow, longhorn, buffalo, elk, and even furs and hides.

NATIVE AMERICAN

Chimayó Trading del Norte
#1 Ranchos Church Plaza
(505) 758-0504
(888) 758-0504
www.chimayotrading.com

This is the Ranchos de Taos location of the Chimayó store (see page 145), specializing in authentic Native American wares, from a nice selection of Mexican pottery to the famous Hispanic Chimayó weavings. The store is located alongside the church of St. Francis of Assisi.

R. B. Ravens
4146 Highway 68
(505) 758-7322
(800) 253-5398
www.rbravens.com

Though mostly a paintings gallery, R. B. Ravens deals in high-quality Native American works, including katsina dolls, pottery, and rugs. This is a great place to check out antique Navajo rugs and pueblo pottery.

SAN FELIPE PUEBLO

North of Albuquerque, San Felipe remains a small, conservative pueblo without many shopping opportunities. Keep an eye out for the small gift shop across from the San Felipe Casino.

SAN ILDEFONSO PUEBLO

Given the fame of Maria Martinez and her black-on-black pottery, you may be surprised at the low-key atmosphere of San Ildefonso Pueblo, just north of Santa Fe. Still, thousands of connoisseurs and curious tourists visit the pueblo every year. A stunning cottonwood tree marks the center of the plaza, and artisans' home-based workshops fan out along its edges. All the shops are in the artisans' homes, so it's a great opportunity to witness pueblo life. Among the best shops are Aguilar and Pena, and the visitor center also offers a few examples of the pueblo's famous wares.

SAN JUAN PUEBLO

Oke Oweenge Arts and Crafts Cooperative
Off Highway 64
(505) 852-2372

This co-op displays the crafts of eight northern pueblos, including redware pottery and textiles of the San Juan. Look for special ceremonial apparel richly decorated, as well as beadwork and silver jewelry.

SANTA ANA PUEBLO

Fifteen minutes north of Albuquerque, visitors can visit Santa Ana only during ceremonial days. At the pueblo-run TaMaYa Crafts Cooperative, keep an eye out for pottery and wooden crosses with straw inlay, a Hispanic craft that was passed along to the Santa Ana people centuries ago.

SANTA CLARA PUEBLO

The characteristic black-on-black pottery of Santa Clara is a favorite of collectors, but the pueblo also boasts weavers and beadworkers. The best bet is to wander the pueblo looking for "Open" signs in the windows, and to buy directly from the craftspeople themselves. Don't miss the fascinating cliff dwellings.

SANTA FE

Santa Fe boasts what is probably the greatest volume of quality traditional crafts in the Southwest. This distinction is due in part to history; Santa Fe has been a crossroads of exchange for thousands of years. The Anasazi Indians traded precious stones, shells, coral, weavings, and other goods with the Plains Indians to the north and the native peoples in present-day Mexico. The Spanish established a major community here, and continued the tradition of exchanging silver, animal hides, and other goods. Finally, the Santa Fe Trail and the railroad brought Anglo influence into the mix. The Santa Fe Trail linked Santa Fe to Independence, Missouri, and was a major trade route of the 1800s. It was mainly used for trade with the Spanish provinces.

Today, Santa Fe is one of the nation's premier artist communities and a true shopper's paradise for fans of southwestern crafts of all three traditions. Expect to pay a little more in Santa Fe for quality crafts; the advantage is having the Southwest's largest selection of goods within just a few square miles.

GENERAL CRAFTS

Conejo Jewelry Creations
122 Grant Avenue
(505) 983-6678
www.conejojewelrycreations.com

With a small but impressive display set up in the lobby of the Grant Corner Inn, Conejo Jewelry is the brainchild of two artisans whose contemporary, chunky necklaces and other adornments owe their heritage to the spirit of the Southwest.

Cutlery of Santa Fe
107 Old Santa Fe Trail
(505) 982-3262
www.cutleryofsantafe.com

Alongside more commercial cutlery from around the world, Cutlery of Santa Fe features a special line of handmade knives, cheese slicers, and other wares inlaid with turquoise, silver, and other stones. Probably the most unique offering is a knife whose handle is crafted of dinosaur bone from Utah. This shop is near the plaza alongside the La Fonda Hotel. Service is curt at best.

The Golden Eye
115 Don Gaspar Avenue
(505) 984-0040
(800) 784-0038
www.goldeneyesantafe.com

With a mysterious Egyptian flair, this tiny jewelry store stands out for the exceptional quality of its handcrafted gold jewelry. Many of the pendants, earrings, and bracelets are inspired by ancient cultures around the world, including that of Native Americans. Prices are commensurate with the quality of these unique pieces.

Jackalope
2820 Cerillos Road
(505) 471-8539
www.jackalope.com

This is one of the Southwest's most memorable shopping experiences. Hidden among a huge selection of cheap and tacky souvenirs lay some nice handmade goods: cool hand-carved wooden table accessories, Christmas ornaments, and the enormous ceramic planters that lie outside the store. This is a great place to sample some of the Southwest's culinary specialties as well, including salsas and chiles.

Kania-Ferrin Gallery
662 Canyon Road
(505) 982-8767

Anyone interested in the art of Native American basketry should include this Canyon Road gallery on his or her must-see list. Owner John Kania is a recognized expert on Native American baskets, and the gallery offers a wide array of quality baskets from the nineteenth century to the present. In addition, he carries Native American works such as Navajo rugs, as well as Hispanic religious crafts, all of which are housed in an historic adobe building. The combination makes this one of the more interesting galleries in the area.

Museum of Fine Arts, Museum Shop
107 West Palace Avenue
(505) 988-6211

This fabulous collection of Native American and Hispanic works is a great place to begin immersing yourself in the craft traditions of the Southwest. The museum shop carries a large array of Native American and Hispanic crafts, and this is one of the few places to pick up fine-quality straw appliqué from the Hispanic tradition.

Museum of International Folk Art, Gift Shop
706 Camino Lejo
(505) 476-1200
www.moifa.org

Before hitting the museum shop, be sure to check out one of the most beautiful displays of New Mexican santos in the region. The Museum of New Mexico Foundation Shops runs museum stores at four of Santa Fe's premier museums: the Museum of International Folk Art, the Palace of the Governors, the Museum of Fine Arts, and the Museum of Indian Arts and Culture. The shops are some of the best places to buy authentic goods. You will rarely find a bargain here . . . just good-quality crafts from New Mexico artisans of all three traditions.

Packard's
61 Old Santa Fe Trail
(505) 983-9241
www.packards-santafe.com

Packard's is one of Santa Fe's most venerable institutions, located on the Plaza for some eighty years. It carries a well-chosen selection of Native American textiles, jewelry, katsinam, and other crafts, as well as Western wear, including handmade belt buckles.

Relics of the Old West
402 Old Santa Fe Trail
(505) 989-7663

Cowboys-and-Indians fans will treasure a visit to Relics of the Old West, which carries an extensive collection of everything from spurs to chaps and high-quality Navajo rugs. Sometimes there are Navajo weavers at work on-site.

Simply Southwestern of Santa Fe
70 East San Francisco Street
(505) 989-8800
www.simplysouthwestern.com

Though many of the items sold in this shop are nothing special, it's worth a stop to view the mind-boggling work of Jon Anderson. Anderson pioneered a technique in which he uses polymer clay to create whimsical animals with so many colors and intricate designs that you want to get as close as you can to examine

all the rich detail. The process is similar to creating millefiori glass, in that it utilizes minuscule canes of different colored clay to create intricate and colorful designs.

HISPANIC

Antique Warehouse

530 South Guadalupe Street
(505) 984-1159
www.antiquewarehouse-santafe.com

If you're in the market for architectural elements like doors, columns, or Spanish colonial antiques, this is the place for quality stuff.

Bosshard Fine Art Furnishings

340 Read Street
(505) 989-9150
www.johnbosshard.com

This is the Santa Fe location of the Taos gallery (see page 161) that offers Spanish colonial antiques and other one-of-a-kind collectibles from several world cultures.

El Rancho de Las Golondrinas, Museum Shop

334 Los Pinos Road
(505) 471-2261
www.golondrinas.org

This unique living-history museum allows you to step back in time to Spanish colonial New Mexico and to experience village life as it was in the early eighteenth century. The museum shop sells a wonderful array of bultos and retablos, as well as other traditional Hispanic New Mexican crafts. The museum is located just south of Santa Fe.

Foreign Traders

202 Galisteo Street
(505) 983-6441
(866) 530-9080
www.foreigntraders.com

This interior-design showcase features many handmade items from Mexico, including milagro charms and santos, hand-hewn bowls made of cottonwood, and wrought iron candlesticks and accessories. Foreign Traders traces its connection to Santa Fe back three generations, making it one of the city's more reputable dealers of Mexican imports.

Hands of America
401 Rodeo Road
(505) 983-5550

This beautiful showroom brings together worn armoires that reek of their Spanish colonial past, religious paintings in elaborate metal frames, saints, altarpieces, architectural elements, and other one-of-a-kind antiques that create a sumptuous display. Restorers on staff can bring your unique antique back to its original condition.

Marc Navarro Gallery
520 Canyon Road
(505) 986-8191

Located along the exclusive stretch of galleries on Canyon Road, the Marc Navarro Gallery specializes in antique Spanish colonial pieces. A handpicked selection of works includes bultos, retablos, milagros, relicarios, jewelry, and an ever-changing collection of truly interesting Hispanic arts.

*Montez Gallery
125 East Palace Avenue, Suites 33 and 34
(505) 982-1828
www.montezsantafe.com

Great values abound on quality bultos and retablos, ex-votos, rustic antique furniture, and unique religious art such as harder-to-find relicarios. The historic Sena Plaza, one of the Southwest's most evocative, makes a beautiful locale for this special little gallery.

Museum of Spanish Colonial Art, Gift Shop
750 Camino Lejo
(505) 982-2226
www.spanishcolonial.org

This is the country's premier museum of Spanish colonial art, and the gift shop is a good choice for picking up quality crafts and reproductions of the works you see in the collection.

Pachamama
223 Canyon Road
(505) 983-4020

A wonderful selection of santos, silver jewelry, Day of the Dead goods, beaded and silver jewelry, Spanish colonial furniture, textiles, retablos, and many other treasures make this gallery a joy to peruse. Many of the works are antiques.

Southwest Spanish Craftsmen
314 South Guadalupe Street
(505) 982-1767
(800) 777-1767
www.southwestspanishcraftsmen.com

Unleash the interior designer within you at this fabulous Santa Fe store. It's hard to find higher-quality Spanish colonial–style chests, armoires, and other rustic furniture. You can also contract a furniture craftsman to design a special set of doors, bookcases, or other architectural element to lend a distinctly Hispanic flavor to your home.

*Todos Santos Chocolatier and Confectioner
125 East Palace Avenue, Suite 31
(505) 982-3855

Gilded chocolate saints, sugar-coated milagros, and sugar skulls make this the best place to stock up for your Day of the Dead celebrations—a treat for the eyes as well as the taste buds!

NATIVE AMERICAN

*Andrea Fisher Fine Pottery
100 West San Francisco Street
(505) 986-1234
www.andreafisherpottery.com

Of the thousands of places to buy pueblo pottery in the Southwest, this one stands out for its quality and selection. Whether you're a serious collector or making a first-time purchase, the well-informed staff at Andrea Fisher can guide you to quality works of all the major tribes of New Mexico and the Southwest.

Case Trading Post at The Wheelwright Museum of the American Indian
704 Camino Lejo
(505) 982-4636
(800) 607-4636
www.casetradingpost.com

One of the most well-done museum shops I've ever seen, the Case Trading Post is the retail arm of The Wheelright Museum of The American Indian. Built to resemble a traditional Navajo trading post, the space offers hundreds of quality Native American crafts to fit any budget, from pottery to jewelry and katsinam.

Eagle Dancer
57 Old Santa Fe Trail
(505) 986-2055

Three floors of Native American crafts await you at Eagle Dancer. Don't miss the pawn vault with some interesting treasures from the 1950s and 1960s.

Indian Arts Research Center
660 Garcia Street
(505) 954-7205

Part of the School of American Research, this scholarly institution promotes and facilitates the work of Native American artisans with a number of fellowships and important community initiatives. Disappointingly, the gift shop carries books and cards instead of Indian crafts, but it's worth a stop to check out one of the Southwest's finest collections of Native American works from prehistory to the present.

Institute of American Indian Art, Museum Shop
108 Cathedral Place
(505) 983-1666
www.iaiancad.org

This is one of the country's leading institutions of Native American culture and one of the largest collections of Native American crafts. The museum store offers a quality selection of Native American pottery, jewelry, Zuni fetishes, and other crafts at prices to fit any budget.

Keshi, the Zuni Connection
227 Don Gaspar Avenue
(505) 989-8728
www.keshi.com

This is one of the region's most reputable dealers of Zuni crafts, specializing in fetishes and fetish jewelry. Ask the helpful staff about other Zuni works you may be less familiar with—interesting works of pottery, beadwork, and other unique pieces. Keshi is endorsed by the Council for Indigenous Arts and Culture.

Kiva Fine Arts
102 East Water Street
(505) 982-4273
www.kivaindianart.com

Though mostly a gallery of paintings and sculpture, Kiva Fine Arts is worth a stop to check out their selection of Native American pottery, katsinam, jewelry, and gourd art.

*Me'Dru
60 East San Francisco Street, #229
(505) 920-2935

I purchased a green turquoise necklace and earrings that I wear all the time in this friendly shop. For excellent service, quality craftsmanship, and fair prices, it is hard to beat this tiny space located on the upper level of the Galeria off the Plaza. This family-owned Native American enterprise gets my vote for one of the best places in the Southwest to buy jewelry. Other family members sell works in the Santa Fe Plaza.

Morning Star Gallery Limited
513 Canyon Road
(505) 982-8187
www.morningstargallery.com

This upscale Canyon Road gallery is one of the country's most important dealers of antique Native American crafts, from pueblo pottery to beadwork, basketry, traditional apparel, jewelry, and other unique pieces. Some tribes outside the Southwest are also represented, including the Inuit and Native Americans from the Pacific Northwest.

Museum of Indian Arts and Culture, Museum Store
710 Camino Lejo
(505) 476-1250
www.miaclab.org

This important collection is one of the nation's most significant repositories of Native American archeological finds, and includes an enormous display of pottery from the Anasazi to the present day. The museum shop offers authentic Native American crafts, from katsina dolls to jewelry, weavings, and baskets.

*Native American Artisans Program
Arcade of the Palace of the Governors, on the Santa Fe Plaza
(505) 476-5112

Authentic wares, reasonable prices, and the chance to interact directly with the artisans

combine to make this one of the most memorable shopping experiences in the Southwest. Under the arcades of Santa Fe's Palace of the Governors, Native American craftspeople spread blankets and set up portable tables and chairs to display a colorful array of wares, mostly pottery and jewelry. Any day of the week you'll find a few dozen craftspeople hawking their wares, but an astonishing nine hundred artisans representing all of New Mexico's native peoples are officially registered to conduct business here.

Rainbow Man
107 East Palace Avenue
(505) 982-8706
www.therainbowman.com

A fabulous colorful courtyard spills over with treasures at the Rainbow Man, one of Santa Fe's oldest Indian trading establishments. In addition to antique jewelry, pottery, and more, it carries an interesting selection of historical photographs of Native Americans.

Santa Fe Indian Trading Company
56 Lincoln Avenue
(505) 984-1364

A tourist trap on one side, this store on the Plaza has a nice gallery on the other side with a good selection of Native American crafts including Zuni fetishes, jewelry, and rugs.

Shalako Indian Store
66 East San Francisco Street, #5
(505) 983-8018
www.shalakoindianstore.com

Located in the Plaza Galeria alongside more touristy shops, this store's glass cases gleam with Indian pawn and contemporary Native American jewelry. It also carries small crafts such as fetishes, beadwork, and storyteller figures, and a staggering array of belts.

Shush Yaz Trading Co.
1048 Paseo de Peralta
(505) 992-0441
www.shushyaz.com

Don Tanner is the fourth generation to work in this business; his great-grandfather traversed northern Arizona on a wagon train and traded with the Navajo. Today, Shush Yaz has made a name for itself with the vast quantity of Indian pawn jewelry, but also Hopi katsina dolls, pottery, baskets, and Navajo rugs. Clean out your attic, bring in your goods, and Don Tanner and company will tell you what they're worth. Shush Yaz also runs a store in Gallup (see page 147).

Wind River Trading Company
113 East San Francisco Street
(505) 989-7062

Wind River offers up one of Santa Fe's largest collections of Indian crafts. The selection of Navajo and Zapotec weavings is particularly impressive.

WESTERN

*Back at the Ranch
209 East Marcy Street
(888)-96BOOTS
www.backattheranch.com

Back at the Ranch gets my vote for the most unique handcrafted cowboy boots in the entire Southwest. And that's saying a lot in this mecca of cowboy wear. Hundreds of colorful boot models line the walls of this upscale boutique. You can pick from a rainbow of colored leathers, including alligator, ostrich, and other exotic hides. Have the boots made to measure in consultation with a member of the expert staff, or schedule a visit with Tyler Beard, one of the West's preeminent boot makers and historians of Western wear. Contact them to learn about designer trunk shows. A pair of boots starts at $695; it takes four to five months to fill a custom order.

The Brown Cow Saddle Blanket Company
Source Design Marketplace
333 Cordova Road
(505) 820-6297
www.thebrowncow.com

If your horse deserves only the best, stop into The Brown Cow Saddle Blanket Company for a handmade woolen saddle blanket starting at about $600. In addition to a grand array of custom-made and stock saddle blankets, the store carries quality horse tack from beaded halters to other accessories I'll bet even the most die-hard equestrians have never fathomed. You can pick up a snazzy riding outfit for yourself while you're there.

Douglas Magnus
905 Early Street
(505) 983-6777
www.douglasmagnus.com

Look for the works of this Santa Fe jewelry artisan on the Hollywood red carpet, as Douglas Magnus is a jeweler to the jet set. It's easy to appreciate the star-studded appeal of his works, truly beautiful contemporary silver and turquoise jewelry based on traditional Native American and Western prototypes. Magnus owns three turquoise mines himself, and has worked the stone for more than thirty years.

Gusterman Silversmiths
126 East Palace, Sena Plaza
(505) 982-8972
www.gusterman.com

Gusterman is worth a visit just to watch Britt

Gusterman and her assistants forging beautiful jewelry in the shop. This workshop-turned-jewelry-store makes up for in magic what it lacks in space. Truly one-of-a-kind pieces are produced here with love, including my favorite: jewelry with unpolished turquoise. It is simply stunning in its understated, rustic beauty.

Liberty Westerns
227 Don Gaspar Avenue
(505) 989-9315

If you want to return home with a truly unique outfit, stop at this shop and order a custom-made suit with Western embroidery and tailoring. The warm showroom displays vintage Western wear, as well as sample custom garments to spark your imagination.

Lucchese Boot Co.
203 West Water Street
(505) 820-1883
(800) 871-1883
www.lucchese.com

The Lucchese family has been handcrafting fine cowboy boots since 1883, when Sam Lucchese immigrated from Italy to America and established the company in San Antonio, Texas. His grandson now carries on the tradition of craftsmanship that has made Lucchese one of the most well-respected "factory" boot makers in the country. Lucchese distributes to Western-wear stores across the country, but this Santa Fe location is a great place to get these top-quality boots.

Montecristi Custom Hat Works
322 McKenzie Street
(505) 983-9598
www.montecristihats.com

This custom hatter can whip up a Panama hat specially made for your head, as well as unique belt buckle sets you'll treasure forever.

Rio Bravo Trading Company
411 South Guadalupe Street
(505) 982-0230

Both serious collectors and first-time visitors will appreciate this store, a true blast from the past. Every square inch of this evocative old-fashioned trading post is covered with remnants of the past—antique spurs, dented cowboy hats, Indian pawn jewelry, worn cowboy boots, gun leather, rawhide chaps, and other small treasures. Owner Randy Rodriguez will gladly share his passion for these relics of the Old West.

Tom Taylor
108 East San Francisco Street
(505) 984-2231
(800) 303-9733
www.tomtaylorbuckles.com

Schedule a forty-five-minute consultation with Jean or Holly Taylor to get a pair of perfectly fitted cowboy boots. You can choose the leather, toe, heel, shanks, and pulls. Then pick out a customized belt and buckle to go with your new boots. Allow six to eight weeks for delivery, and expect to pay $350 and up for a pair of boots. Simple sterling silver belt buckles start at around $250. Models inlaid with stone, or crafted of 14-karat gold, go for $500 to $1,000. The service is excellent in this unique and authentic Santa Fe shop.

SANTO DOMINGO PUEBLO

Santo Domingo is located near the major turquoise mines of New Mexico twenty-five miles south of Santa Fe, so it makes sense that its major craft tradition is jewelry. These pueblo artisans are especially known for heishi, the flattened turquoise beads usually strung in stacks on long strands. Look for the work of Parrot and Wolves, and the Coriz family, which crafts necklaces with beautiful turquoise charms.

SHIPROCK

NATIVE AMERICAN

Foutz Trading Company
Highway 64
(505) 368-5790
www.foutztrade.com

The Foutz family traces its trading roots back some hundred years, and today operates several trading posts on the Navajo reservation as well as a wholesale rug division. The Shiprock store carries a variety of Navajo crafts, with a special emphasis on weavings.

TAOS

Second only to Santa Fe in terms of its status as an artist community, Taos is another excellent center for crafts of Native American, Hispanic, and Western traditions.

GENERAL CRAFTS

Bryans Gallery
121 Kit Carson Road
(505) 758-9407
www.bryansgallery.com

In a bright gallery space, Bryans Gallery assembles an eclectic collection of traditional Native American works along with funky contemporary crafts. Modern twists on Indian ceremonial masks and katsina dolls are particularly refreshing, and the display cases offer one of the region's largest selections of Zuni fetishes.

Furniture Design of Taos
22 La Ceja Road
(505) 776-5007
www.furnituredesignoftaos.com

The exquisite woodwork of Northern New Mexico is represented in this showroom of custom and stock furniture, now located in Valdez, nine miles North of Taos. Rustic, functional pieces with folk art motifs are the hallmark of husband-and-wife woodworking pair Bob Bresnahan and Emily Zopf, who will create a custom piece to suit your style.

La Unica Cosa and Starr Gallery
117 Paseo del Pueblo Norte
(505) 758-3065
(800) 748-1756
www.zapotec.com
www.zapotecmarket.com
www.starrgallery.com

A beautiful and evocative courtyard lures passersby into the rug-filled galleries of La Unica Cosa. Handmade wool rugs, wall hang-

ings, pillows, and other textiles fill the rooms with a warm and inviting atmosphere. Many of the weavings are made by Zapotec Indians in the mountains near Oaxaca, Mexico. Prices are high but so is the quality.

*Millicent Rogers Museum, Museum Shop
1504 Millicent Rogers Road
(505) 758-2462
www.millicentrogers.org

This unique collection houses one of the Southwest's most important assemblages of Hispanic and Native American crafts. After ending a relationship with Hollywood super-star Clark Gable, Millicent Rogers took off to quiet Taos to nurse a broken heart. There the Standard Oil heiress amassed one of the country's most impressive collections of Native American and Hispanic crafts, all in the few years between 1947 and 1956, when the museum opened its doors. In addition to visiting the museum, check out the museum shop, which carries Native American weavings and pottery, Hispanic santos, and jewelry stylish enough to live up to the standards of Millicent Rogers herself.

Taos Beads and Design
100-B South Taos Plaza
(505) 751-7475

If the artisan within is itching to get out, this is a great place to buy supplies. Trays of beads fill this small retail space, and finished jewelry on the walls provides inspiration. In addition to glass, coral, and stones of all types, look for turquoise and other stones used in Native American jewelry.

HISPANIC

Bosshard Fine Art Furnishings
112 Camino de la Placita
(505) 751-9445
www.johnbosshard.com

Amid exotic furnishings from India and other faraway lands, John Bosshard carries some of the most impressive pieces of Spanish colonial furniture in the region. Check his shop for the current selection of chests, sideboards, chairs, and architectural pieces. There is a

sister store in Santa Fe as well (see page 154).

El Venado Import Shop
Cabot Plaza
108 Kit Carson Road
(505) 751-7718

This lovely store carries an impressive selection of copper and ceramic sinks, rustic furniture, silver jewelry, Talavera pottery, and other handmade decorative items from Mexico.

Harwood Museum, Museum Shop
238 Ledoux Street
(505) 758-9826
www.harwoodmuseum.org

Part of the University of New Mexico, this varied and eclectic museum carries an impressive collection of antique and contemporary Hispanic furniture, tinware, retablos, and bultos in its Hispanic Traditions gallery. Check out the museum shop for quality crafts and reproductions of some of the museum's pieces.

NATIVE AMERICAN

*Blue Rain Gallery
117 South Plaza
(505) 751-0066
www.blueraingallery.com

A favorite of collectors, Blue Rain is mostly a fine arts gallery but also carries high-quality baskets, pottery, katsina dolls, and other Native American works. This is a great place to find works steeped in tradition but with a more contemporary spirit.

Buffalo Dancer
103 East Plaza, #A
(505) 758-8718

This is one of Taos's more reputable dealers of Native American arts, and the uniqueness of the shop's offerings is one of the reasons. In addition to some more affordable concha belts, buckles, and jewelry, it also sells some museum-quality antiques out of reach of all except the most affluent collectors. Other one-of-a-kind items are products made from buffalo, including pots, belts, turquoise knives, leather goods, and drums.

Carson House Shop
117 Kit Carson Road
(505) 758-0113
www.carsonhouseshop.com

Amid more commercial gift items you'll find
some quality pieces of pueblo pottery, including some nice examples of horsehair pottery,
jewelry, katsina dolls, and other works.

*Pueblo Drums
110 Paseo del Pueblo Norte
(505) 758-7929
(888) 412-3786
www.pueblodrums.com

These high-quality ceremonial drums are
made by the Philip Martinez family, Native
American artisans. The drums are made in
nearby Taos Pueblo, and come in small and
large versions with hand-painted motifs.

Smoke Signals
121 North Plaza
(505) 737-9227

Taos Pueblo artisan Dean Johnson creates
handcrafted peace pipes and other Native
American works at this tiny shop on the main
plaza in Taos.

Southwest Moccasin & Drum
803 Paseo del Pueblo Norte
(505) 758-9332
www.swnativecrafts.com

Southwest Moccasin & Drum is a great place
to pick up Native American drums and other
musical instruments, as well as quality beaded
moccasins, many of which are handmade.

Taos Drums
3956 Highway 68
(800) 424-3786

Drums of every size line the shelves of Taos
Drums—some are hand-painted, some are left
with the natural look of the hides. These
Indian-made drums are so well regarded that
bands like Pearl Jam and Fleetwood Mac have
sought them out. In the style of a factory
showroom, browse not only drums but lamp
shades and other goodies made of rawhide.
The staff is not the friendliest, but Taos
Drums is an institution and worth a stop.
Look for the giant tepees along Route 68 as
you approach Taos from the south.

Taos Moccasin Company Factory Outlet
216-B Paseo del Pueblo Sur
(505) 751-0032
(800) 747-7025
www.taosmocs.com

Although the company's shoes are factory
produced, Taos Moccasin is one of the more
well-respected traditional footwear companies
distributing old-style moccasins in stores
throughout the country. In this factory outlet
you can find some good bargains on moccasins made of elk, deer, and moose hides, as
well as some nice hand-beaded purses.

Weaving Southwest
216-B Paseo del Pueblo Norte
(505) 758-0433
(800) 765-1272
www.weavingsouthwest.com

This fabulous tapestry gallery is a great place to watch weaving in action and to sample the best weaving traditions of the Southwest. In addition to representing some of the most skilled artisans at work today, the gallery also supplies the weaving community with hand-dyed yarns for rugs and blankets.

TAOS PUEBLO

Architecturally, Taos Pueblo is one of the most interesting Native American settlements in the United States. My recommendation is to spend at least half a day exploring Taos Pueblo, as many artisans occupy the nooks and crannies of this conglomeration of mud-and-straw adobe dwellings constructed between 1000 and 1450. In terms of crafts, the artisans are known for their glittery micaceous pottery and painted drums. You can buy with confidence from artisans hawking wares from their homes and at makeshift stands around the pueblo. At the entrance ask where to find the following excellent crafts-people: Jacqueline Gala (jewelry), Dolly "Sunflower" Luha (drums), and Judy Ann Stribling (silver).

TESUQUE

GENERAL CRAFTS

Richard J. Fisher Tinworks
Griegos Arroyo Road
(505) 989-4227
www.fishertinworks.com

Beautiful frames for pictures and mirrors are the specialty of this artisan in off-the-beaten-path Tesuque.

Tesuque Glassworks
1510 Bishops Lodge Road
(505) 988-2165

Off a winding country road in the woods

north of Santa Fe is Tesuque Glassworks. Six different artisans demonstrate the art of glass-blowing in the open studio. It is located alongside the Shidoni bronze foundry, with its picturesque outdoor sculpture garden.

VANDERWAGON

NATIVE AMERICAN

Joe Milo's White Water Trading Co.
Highway 602
(505) 778-5314
(888) 563-6456
www.joemilo.com

Seventeen miles south of Gallup, Joe Milo's White Water Trading Co. plies its rural setting to create a traditional trading post atmosphere. It sells crafts of the Zuni, Navajo, Hopi, Acoma, and other New Mexico pueblos.

WATERFLOW

NATIVE AMERICAN

Bob French Navajo Rugs
3459 Highway 64
(505) 598-5621
www.bobfrenchs.com

Over the last generation, Bob French and family have made a name for themselves in the Four Corners region as dealers of high-quality Navajo rugs of all the major weaving styles, from "Ganado red" to Teec Nos Pos and Two Gray Hills. They also carry other Navajo crafts, including jewelry and pottery.

Hogback Trading Company
3221 Highway 64
(505) 598-5154

In a hogan-shaped building, Hogback Trading offers a wide variety of Navajo crafts, including baskets, jewelry, rugs, and other works.

ZIA PUEBLO

The Zia Cultural Center in Zia Pueblo offers weavings, sculpture, and pottery featuring the distinctive Zia bird, which resembles a road-runner and swiftly bears prayers to the gods.

ZUNI PUEBLO

Zuni, famous for its small animal fetishes and jewelry made of mosaic and inlay, is a short trip from Gallup or Albuquerque. Zuni is the largest of New Mexico's nineteen pueblos, and 80 percent of its population is involved in the craft industry. You can buy directly from artisans scattered in homes across the pueblo or from one of the tribe-owned organizations listed below.

*Pueblo of Zuni Arts & Crafts

1222 State Highway 53
(505) 782-5531
(866) 515-7675
www.puebloofzuniarts.com

This tribe-owned store in Zuni Pueblo is my favorite place to purchase authentic Zuni fetishes, jewelry, and pottery. The pleasant space is filled with authentic traditional crafts of the Zuni people—fetishes, jewelry, katsina dolls, beadwork, and pottery. The management fosters the tribe's craftsmanship and promotes it outside the pueblo. Each piece is signed by the artisan.

Turquoise Village

Highway 53
(505) 782-5521
(800) 748-2405
www.turquoisevillage.com

Located on Highway 53 in the center of Zuni Pueblo, Turquoise Village is an excellent choice for locating that perfect Zuni fetish, necklace, bracelet, or other piece of jewelry. This tribe-owned enterprise also supplies many of the Zuni artisans with the raw materials to practice their craft, from shell to coral, lapis, silver, and gold. It also carries a few crafts from Hopi artisans.

Zuni Craftsman Cooperative

1177 West Highway 53
(505) 782-4425

This tribe-owned artist cooperative offers fetishes and jewelry from a variety of Zuni craftspeople and promotes Zuni craftsmanship.

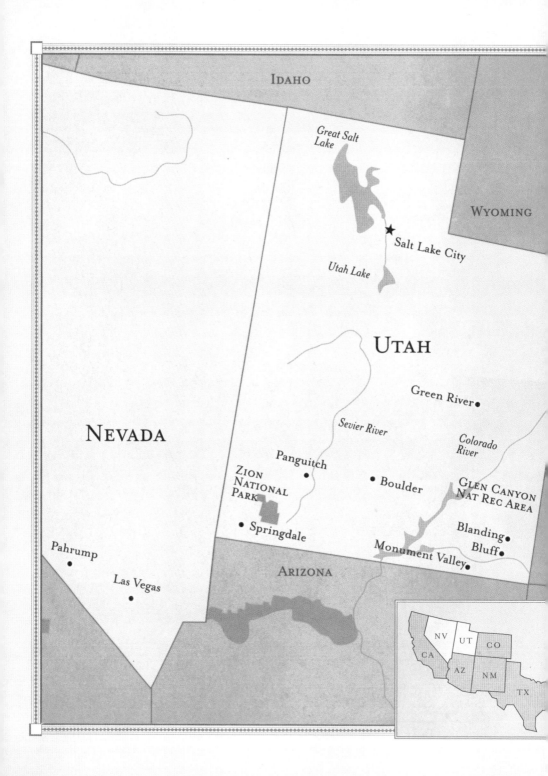

SOUTHERN NEVADA
and UTAH

S outhern Nevada and Utah give new meaning to the term "Wild West." Historically these regions stood at the fringes of civilization, and with the notable exception of Las Vegas, still today take time to get to and are little populated. Roads are few and far between as they wind through this landscape of vertical cliffs, remarkable rock formations, inhospitable deserts, and vast, desolate canyons. The so-called Colorado Plateau of Utah is a strange and stunning landscape with some of the most unusual scenery in the country, sparsely inhabited by both plants and people. Southeastern Utah contains all of the state's national parks, including Zion, Canyonlands, and Bryce Canyon.

The first inhabitants of these lands were the Anasazi and Fremont Indians, and later the Shoshone, Ute, and Navajo. They crafted baskets and pottery, and lived in meager settlements throughout the land. The Spanish colonists' agenda was less successful here, as they did not find the Indian settlements suitable for missionary work, and their forays into this region were sporadic and short lived. Spanish, Russian, and eventually Anglo explorers traveled through the territory trying to find good overland routes to California, but none of them ever really settled there.

It's no wonder that these rugged areas attracted the nineteenth century's legendary "mountain men," mavericks who turned their backs on the civilized world to live their dream of surviving in the wilderness alongside Native Americans. These mountain men were among the first Anglos to explore the beautiful canyons and rock formations—formed by geological forces millions of years ago—that characterize southeastern Utah. These pioneering Anglos were captivated by this wild land and its people; some learned the Native American tongues, married into Indian families, and lived off the land, in part by trapping beavers and other creatures, and trading in furs. Eventually the call of the wild also lured gamblers, prostitutes, and merchants to southern Nevada, where they established brothels and casinos that still thrive today.

Craft shopping in these regions can be a tricky business, as trading establishments are few and far between, and many retail shops sell more tourist souvenirs than quality, handcrafted goods. Still, the region is home to a few of the Southwest's most historically significant trading posts that still operate as brokers for high-quality Native American works. The hallmark of the trading posts of southern Nevada and Utah is that they are one-stop shopping experiences: you can have a meal, get a haircut, pick up groceries, fill up your car with gas, and if you're lucky, buy some nice Navajo jewelry while you're there.

Listings preceded by an asterisk (*) denote my personal favorites.

NEVADA

ELY

NATIVE AMERICAN

Smoke Signals Indian Trading Post
598 Aultman Street
(775) 289-4848
www.nevadaweb.com/smoke

Indian-owned and Indian-operated, Smoke
Signals specializes in Native American jewelry
and beadwork. Occasionally you can watch
artisans crafting pieces on-site.

LAS VEGAS

I would not make a special trip to Las Vegas to
shop for crafts, but if you're there anyway and
have hit it big at the blackjack table, the following stores are good places to drop some cash.

GENERAL CRAFTS

Ray's Beaver Bag
725 Las Vegas Boulevard South
(702) 386-8746

A favorite hangout for locals, Ray's Beaver Bag
is an 1800s-style trading post that specializes
in anything you might need to survive in the
Wild West. The shelves and walls are filled to
the brim with camp cookware, hand-sewn
beaver-skin bags, cattle skulls, and raccoon
hats. The owner is an enthusiast of the legendary "mountain men" of the Old West, and
attracts a fair amount of local color in this
unique landmark that transports you miles
away from the glitz of the Las Vegas strip.

West of Santa Fe
3500 Las Vegas Boulevard South
(702) 737-1993
www.westofsantafe.com

Inside the Forum at Caesar's Palace, West of
Santa Fe offers a few good handcrafted finds
among more commercially produced items.
The shop carries some antiques, so on any
given day you might find a dusty pair of old
chaps, spurs, or other Western memorabilia.
There is also some nice Native American jewelry and a few good pueblo pots.

UTAH

BLANDING

NATIVE AMERICAN

Hatch Trading Post
County Road 414/412
No telephone

The Hatch Trading Post is one of the authentic trading posts of the early twentieth century set up to trade furs and other goods between Anglos and Native Americans. Today, in an adobe roadside building, there is a small selection of Native American wares alongside a display of candy bars and a cooler full of soda.

Purple Sage Trading Post
790 South Main Street
(435) 678-3620
www.purplesagetradingpost.com

This warm, inviting space displays some of the best of Navajo craftsmanship, from textiles to jewelry. There are also other tribes represented, namely Hopi, Zuni, and Santo Domingo. Herbal supplements are another specialty, just in case you left yours at home. This small pioneer town in the heart of some of America's most beautiful natural attractions has retained the flavor of yesteryear and is in close proximity to the Navajo nation.

BLUFF

NATIVE AMERICAN

Twin Rocks Trading Post
913 East Navajo Twins Drive
(435) 672-2341
(800) 526-3448
www.twinrocks.com

Located about twenty-five miles north of the Navajo reservation, Twin Rocks Trading Post amasses a quality collection of jewelry, katsina dolls, and pottery. The basket and rug selection is particularly good, and the friendly staff is more than happy to chat about the inventory.

BOULDER

NATIVE AMERICAN

Burr Trail Trading Park Post & Grill
Highway 12 and The Burr Trail
(435) 335-7565

The Burr Trail Trading Post is a good pit stop in this one-horse town. After downing a plate of eggs or pancakes, head over to the trading post. Most of the goods are kitschy, but there is some nice Native American jewelry.

GREEN RIVER

NATIVE AMERICAN

MOKI Trading Post
17 East Main Street
(435) 564-8330

Bypass the cheesy souvenirs for the good examples of katsina dolls, pueblo pottery, moccasins, and silver jewelry.

MONUMENT VALLEY

NATIVE AMERICAN

Goulding's Yellow Ribbon Gift Shop
(435) 727-3231
www.gouldings.com

Harry and Leone Goulding founded a trading post on this remote mesa in 1928 to trade food and other supplies with the Navajo in

exchange for jewelry, rugs, and other crafts. Goulding's played a key historical role in connecting Monument Valley with the Hollywood film industry, as the Gouldings lured Hollywood director John Ford there in the 1930s. Today, Monument Valley continues to be a hot spot for movies and TV commercials. The Gouldings' enclave includes a hotel, campground, theater, and grocery store; it even has its own landing strip. The gift shop carries authentic Navajo rugs, jewelry, and pottery alongside typical souvenirs.

PANGUITCH

NATIVE AMERICAN

Bryce Canyon Trading Post
2938 East Highway 12
(435) 676-2688
www.color-country.net/brycetp

A member of the Indian Arts and Crafts Association, this is a good choice for quality Navajo jewelry and other crafts, including

antique Indian pawn items. Look for the chile ristras—dried chiles on a string—hanging in front of the store.

Red Canyon Indian Store
3279 Highway 12
(435) 676-2690
www.redcanyon.net

At this jack-of-all-trades store, you can buy everything from cheap souvenirs to T-shirts, picnic supplies, and authentic Navajo rugs that will set you back thousands of dollars. There are also a few other quality Native American crafts.

SPRINGDALE

GENERAL CRAFTS

Frontier Plunder Antiques
1200 Zion Park Boulevard
(435) 772-3045

If you're lucky you might score a genuine pair

of antique cowboy spurs, gun leather, horse tack, or Native American baskets, jewelry, or pottery. Also keep an eye out for more contemporary Native American works at this wonderland of Wild West treasures.

NATIVE AMERICAN

Big Chief Trading Post
694 Zion Park Boulevard
(435) 772-3334

Billed as the only place in twenty miles to get your hair cut, coiffure is not the only attraction at the Big Chief Trading Post. It also carries antique and contemporary Native American jewelry and other quality crafts.

Majestic View Lodge, Steakhouse, and Saloon
2400 Zion Park Boulevard
(435) 772-0665
(866) 772-0665
www.majesticviewlodge.com

The name says it all . . . well, almost. In addition to a nice lodge, steakhouse, saloon, and even wildlife museum, there's a trading post where you can pick up some quality Native American baskets, pottery, and other crafts.

Tribal Arts
291 Zion Park Boulevard
(435) 772-3353
www.tribalartszion.com

Located near the entrance to Zion National Park, Tribal Arts carries a good selection of Native American crafts from many tribes. The selection of hand-woven baskets is particularly nice.

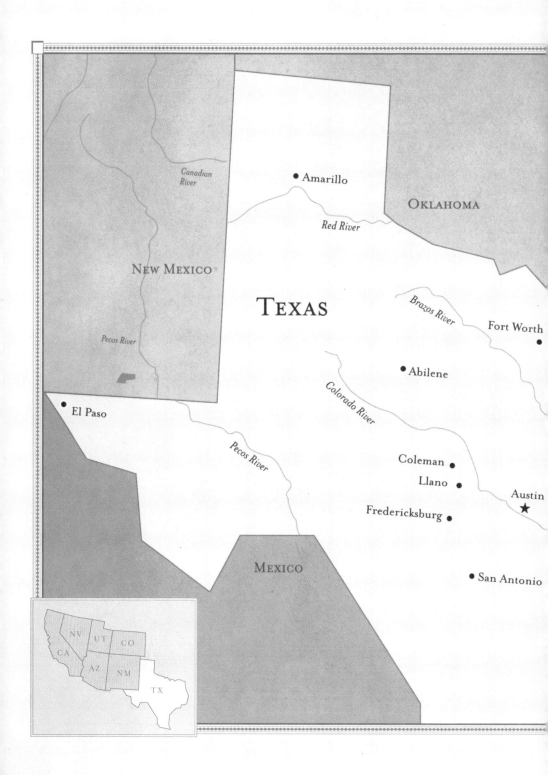

WEST TEXAS

The Mansos, Piro, and Tigua were among the earliest Native American inhabitants of what is now West Texas. The fertile riverbed of the Rio Grande made for a perfect spot for agriculture and hunting. The Spanish set up camp in El Paso in the sixteenth century, one of its earliest colonial cities in what is now the United States, and it became a major stop on the road from Mexico City to Santa Fe. The Spanish established several significant missions in West Texas and established ranching as a major industry in the service of the Spanish crown.

The Mexican-American War kicked off at the Alamo at San Antonio in 1835. When the war ended, the United States claimed Texas and made it the country's twenty-eighth state. The government granted land to Anglo settlers for establishing farms and ranches in this vast land. The arrival of the railroad and more industrial trades such as copper mining brought Texas into the modern age. Cowboy and ranch culture made an indelible mark on West Texas, and Anglo and Hispanic ranchers influenced one another in their attire and equestrian accoutrements.

Nowhere in the Southwest is the selection and quality of cowboy crafts greater than in West Texas. Excellent makers of boots, saddles, and spurs thrive in small shops across the state. Hispanic crafts are also plentiful and affordable, especially in the border towns such as El Paso.

Listings preceded by an asterisk (*) denote my personal favorites.

ABILENE

WESTERN

Bell Custom Boots
2118 North Treadway Boulevard
(325) 677-0632

Alan Bell is a one-man band operating out of
a small shop in Abilene. A pair of boots,
made with the meticulous attention to detail
that has brought him renown in the Western-
wear industry, takes six to eight months to
craft.

AMARILLO

WESTERN

Beck Cowboy Boots
723 South Georgia Street
(806) 373-1600
www.beckboots.com

Choose from ready-made or custom-fitted
cowboy boots at this Amarillo institution,
founded in 1916. Choose your own toe, heel,
vamp, pulls, and height, as well as patterns
and stitching details. Prices start at around
$500 for a basic model that takes several
weeks, or up to three months or more for a
custom pair. If you can't make it to Amarillo
in person, call for a "fit kit" that includes
a foam form for making an impression of
your foot.

*Campbell's Bits and Spurs
6408 River Road
(806) 381-0873
www.campbellspurs.com

This is one of Texas's foremost sources for
quality, handcrafted, tradition-steeped spurs
and bits. Robert and Leo Campbell collabo-
rate to create innovative and beautiful
examples of spurs of silver overlay on steel.
Look for other unique pieces of metalwork,
including belt buckles, conchas, and personalized hoof picks. A pair of spurs starts at
about $250.

Oliver Saddle Shop
3016 Plains Boulevard
(806) 372-7562
www.oliversaddle.com

This shop specializing in custom-made saddles is now in its fourth generation, and produces about a hundred saddles a year.
Customers wait six to eight months for a custom order and pay $2,000 to $3,000,
depending on the labor involved. In addition
to saddles, Oliver also makes spur straps,
chaps, saddlebags, and other leather accessories. The small showroom displays choice
pieces of work, as well as cowboy accessories.

Western Leather Craft Boot
1950 Civic Circle
(806) 355-0174

This custom-boot-making family is now in its
fourth generation of operation, and is known
for its fancy inlays and colorful patterns. A
pair of boots starts at around $600 and takes
about three months to craft.

AUSTIN

NATIVE AMERICAN

Turquoise Trading Post
6103 Burnet Road
(512) 323-5011
www.texasttp.com

This is one of Austin's best sources for quality
Native American crafts, from Acoma pottery
to Zuni fetishes, but exquisite jewelry of
turquoise and coral is the main reason to
make a stop.

WESTERN

Capitol Saddlery
1614 Lavaca Street
(512) 478-9309
www.capitolsaddlery.com

Custom saddles, horse tack, boots, belts, and
other leather accessories are the specialty of
Capitol Saddlery. It's worth a trip to the
showroom just to marvel at the variety of saddles on display.

Texas Traditions
2222 College Avenue
(512) 443-4447

A Vermont native transplanted to Texas, Lee Miller, owner of Texas Traditions, makes gorgeous custom boots with some of the most intricate tooling I've ever seen. The intensive labor and demand for his work (he's made boots for Sting and Lyle Lovett) mean there's a fifteen-month wait for a pair of boots and a starting price of about $1,000.

C O L E M A N

W E S T E R N

Tex Robin
115 West Eighth Street
(325) 625-5556
www.texrobinboots.com

There's nothing on the shelves in this second-generation boot maker's shop. That's because Tex Robin specializes in custom-made, top-of-the-line cowboy boots that start at around $795. Stop in for a chat with Tex Robin and experience West Texas's famous local color.

E L   P A S O

El Paso is a major center for southwestern crafts of the Hispanic and Western traditions. The downtown area is a great place to start, and if you're in the market for custom cowboy boots, El Paso is a premier destination.

H I S P A N I C

Butterfield Trading Post
6669 Gateway West
(915) 771-7723
www.butterfieldtrading.com

Hispanic handmade wares, including wrought iron and weavings, are offered at great values in this open-air market of southwestern crafts.

Galeria San Ysidro
801 Texas Avenue
(915) 544-4444

Collectors take note! The Galeria San Ysidro is a three-floor emporium of traditional Hispanic craftsmanship that takes up an entire city block. With a reputation as a gold mine of rustic furniture, wrought iron, and decorative items, as well as antiques, you never know what you'll find. A few works from Africa and the Middle East are thrown in for spice.

W E S T E R N

Arditti Alligator
1109 Wyoming
(877) 273-4884
www.ardittialligator.com

Boot connoisseurs will recognize the sterling silver logo built into the heel of boots made by Arditti Alligator as a stamp of quality. Thomas Yves Arditti specializes in alligator and exotic leathers, some of the most prized in the world. Famous wearers include Jack Nicholson and Mikhail Gorbachev.

Austin-Hall Boot Co.
230 Chelsea Street
(915) 771-6113

Pick from one of fifty base models, select the leather, choose a toe and top, then decide on a color, and you've got a custom pair of boots at a good value.

CABoots
501 and 505 South Cotton
(915) 544-1855
www.caboots.com

CABoots has been crafting top-quality hand-made cowboy boots for four generations, and it is a favorite of several rock stars. Also created are costume boots suitable for pirates, *Star Wars* characters, and Civil War re-enactors. Boots range in price from $200 to $2,000.

Lucchese Boots Outlet
6601 Montana Avenue, Suite L
(915) 778-8060

I'm a big fan of Lucchese boots and bargains, so this outlet store is right up my alley. Lucchese has been in business since the 1880s and still insists on using handcrafted processes despite its growth into one of the country's great "manufactured" boot operations. Prices that are 50 percent off retail make this place a must-stop for boot lovers.

Rocketbuster Boots
115 South Anthony Street
(915) 541-1300
www.rocketbuster.com

Rocketbuster Boots is worth a stop just to marvel at its showroom, which is part kitsch, part Texas legend, as well as to have a gander at the supposed "World's Largest Boots" displayed there. These are some of the Southwest's most funky and colorful boots, so be prepared to have some fun. Rocketbuster sells both stock and custom styles. Either way, prepare to pay at least $1,000. Oprah Winfrey and Steven Spielberg are among Rocketbuster's clients.

Stallion Boot & Belt Co.
100 North Cotton Street
(915) 532-6268
www.stallionboots.com

Fashion-conscious boot shoppers will want to check out Stallion Boots, makers of some of the best products on the market. Stallion distributes through some high-end retailers around the country and even collaborated with Italian design house Dolce & Gabbana on a line of elaborate cowboy boots. Expect to pay at least $900 for a custom-made pair.

FORT WORTH

WESTERN

M. L. Leddy
2455 North Main Street
(817) 624-3149

M. L. Leddy has been in the boot business since the 1920s and is known for his trademark fancy stitch pattern. Also look for the work of Cindy Jarrott, an excellent artisan who creates custom belts, conchas, and tack accessories.

The Maverick Fine Western Wear and Saloon
100 East Exchange Avenue
(800) 282-1315

Take a break from shopping at this colorful emporium of traditional Western wear, and saunter up to the old-fashioned wooden bar in the Maverick's re-created saloon. The Maverick is a main attraction in the Fort Worth Stockyards.

National Cowgirl Museum and Hall of Fame Gift Shop
1720 Gendy Street
(817) 336-4475
(800) 476-FAME

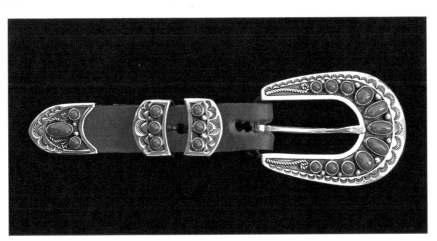

This unique museum honors the women of the Wild West and their historical exploits. The museum shop offers a few high-quality, authentic cowgirl hats in the $500 to $800 range.

Ponder Boot Company
2358 North Main Street
(817) 626-3523
www.ponderboot.com

Former president Ronald Reagan kicked around in boots crafted by the Ponder Boot Company, as has Robert Redford. Jose de la luz Ramirez is the head artisan, considered one of the foremost boot makers in the country. Offering no stock styles, Ponder focuses exclusively on custom-made designs.

FREDERICKSBURG

WESTERN

Texas Jack's
117 North Adams Street
(830) 997-3213
www.texasjacks.com

Occupying an old livery stable, this emporium of Western wear stocks reproductions of typical gear from the late 1800s: double-button shirts, wide-brimmed hats, even a wide selection of firearms.

LEAGUE CITY

NATIVE AMERICAN

Eagle Dancer Gallery
Interstate 45 South
(281) 332-6028
www.eagledancergallery.com

Eagle Dancer stocks a wide selection of Native American pottery, jewelry, fetishes, Hopi katsina dolls, and other miscellaneous objects. Look for examples of beautiful Plains Indian beadwork.

LLANO

WESTERN

Nailhead Spur Company
701 Ford Street

(325) 247-2589
(877) 813-3811
www.nailheadspur.com

This operation sells both stock and custom-made spurs. It carries many accurate reproductions of historical styles, such as California, roping, Pecos, and others. Although the spurs are the main attraction here, Nailhead Spur also crafts cowboy-themed lamps, fire screens, gates, and other decorative items.

MERCEDES

WESTERN

Camargo's Handmade Boots
710 Highway 83
(956) 565-6457

Exotic leathers and imaginative images grace the handmade works of Henry Camargo, a boot maker with an artist's heart. Considering the uniqueness of the products the prices are reasonable, starting at under $300.

Cavazos Boots
302 Second Street
(956) 565-0753

Vicente Cavazos is well known in this Texas border town and beyond for the special decorative inlays and overlays on his colorful boots, which are made by hand, one at a time.

SAN ANTONIO

NATIVE AMERICAN

Gallery of the Southwest
13485 Blanco Road, #197
(210) 493-3344
www.galleryofthesouthwest.com

This gallery has a strong collection of antique and contemporary Native American crafts, from Navajo weavings to Zuni fetishes and katsinam.

WESTERN

*Little's Boots
110 Division Avenue
(210) 923-2221
www.davelittleboots.com

This is probably my favorite of Texas's many excellent handcrafted boot makers, mainly because of the leathers that are so highly buffed they resemble polished wood. Founded by the current owner's grandfather in 1915, Dave Little and about a dozen assistants run this little shop. The boots are renowned for their intricate styling and top-quality craftsmanship.

CALENDAR OF SOUTHWESTERN CRAFT FESTIVALS AND EVENTS

The Southwest hosts an impressive number and variety of annual events in which handmade goods take center stage. These gatherings are a great way to soak up the region's rich cultural traditions and to come face-to-face with individual artisans who you may not have the chance to meet otherwise.

Crafts play a role at virtually all Native American sacred festivals and feast days. Visitors are always welcome to these events, but be sure to contact the pueblo beforehand to ask about etiquette. Many of these events are spiritual rituals and each pueblo observes its own rules about taking photographs, participating in the festivities, and other regulations. You may have to pay a fee to attend some events.

TELEPHONE NUMBERS OF NEW MEXICO'S PUEBLOS

Acoma . . . . (800) 747-0181

Cochití . . . . (505) 465-2244

Isleta. . . . . (505) 869-3111

Jemez . . . . (505) 834-7235

Jicarilla Apache . . . . (505) 759-3242

Laguna . . . . (505) 552-6654

Nambé . . . . (505) 455-2036

Navajo Nation . . . . (928) 871-7941

Picuris . . . . (505) 587-2519

Pojoaque . . . . (505) 455-3334

San Felipe . . . . (505) 867-3381

San Ildefonso. . . . . (505) 455-2273

San Juan. . . . . (505) 852-4400

Sandia . . . . (505) 867-3317

Santa Ana . . . . (505) 867-3301

Santa Clara . . . . (505) 753-7326

Santo Domingo . . . . (505) 465-2214

Taos. . . . . (505) 758-1028

Tesuque. . . . . (505) 983-2667

Zia . . . . (505) 867-3304

Zuni. . . . . (505) 782-7000

Many local festivals offer good values on traditional handmade goods. Here are the major festivals in which handcrafted products play a key role. Dates and locations are subject to change, so call ahead to confirm the details. Listings preceded by an asterisk (*) denote my personal favorites.

JANUARY

ALL MONTH

NEW MEXICO
PUEBLO FEAST DAYS

(505) 843-7270

From January 1 to 25, most of the pueblos sponsor cultural dances and other events in which crafts figure prominently. Contact the pueblos directly for a schedule of events.

MID-JANUARY

PHOENIX, AZ
HIGH NOON SHOW AND AUCTION

Phoenix Civic Plaza

(310) 202-9010

www.highnoon.com

This fabulous exhibition of more than three hundred dealers of Western Americana showcases everything from ropes to saddles and cowboy gear.

MID-JANUARY

DENVER, CO
NATIONAL WESTERN STOCK SHOW
AND RODEO

(303) 297-1166

Organizers claim this is the world's largest rodeo and livestock show, with Western crafts a prominent feature.

FEBRUARY

EARLY FEBRUARY

SCOTTSDALE, AZ
INDIAN ARTISTS OF AMERICA SHOW

(866) 398-2226

www.indianartsofamerica.com

This event showcases the work of more than a hundred Native American artists in a two-day show.

MID-FEBRUARY

CASA GRANDE, AZ
FEBRUARY FESTIVAL AT O'ODHAM TASH

(520) 836-4723

This three-day gathering features Native American crafts and craft judging, alongside ceremonial dances, powwows, and parades.

MID-FEBRUARY

TUBAC, AZ
TUBAC FESTIVAL OF THE ARTS
(520) 398-2704
www.tubacaz.com

A celebration of local craftsmanship is the focus of this annual event.

LATE FEBRUARY

TUCSON, AZ
LA FIESTA DE LOS VAQUEROS
(800) 964-5662
www.tucsonrodeo.com

A rodeo-and-cowboy-themed festival highlighting Tucson's Hispanic and Western heritage is the hallmark of this annual event.

LATE FEBRUARY

TUCSON, AZ
SOUTHWEST INDIAN ART FAIR
Arizona State Museum
(520) 621-6302

www.statemuseum.arizona.edu/events/swiaf/swiaf.shtml

The University of Arizona serves as the setting for this gathering of more than two hundred Native American craftspeople. Watch demonstrations, hear live music, and sample Native American dishes in addition to shopping for good deals on authentic crafts.

MARCH

FIRST WEEKEND

PHOENIX, AZ
*HEARD MUSEUM GUILD ANNUAL INDIAN FAIR & MARKET
(602) 251-0255
www.heard.org

This is the premier institution of Native American heritage and history, and its annual event—held on the grounds of the lovely museum—showcases the work of more than three hundred Native American artisans. In addition, there is music, food, and dance.

MID-MARCH

ORGAN PIPE CACTUS NATIONAL MONUMENT, AZ
O'ODHAM DAY
(520) 387-6849
www.nps.gov/orpi/

The dramatic Organ Pipe Cactus National Monument (OPCNM) serves as a backdrop for a celebration of the traditions of the local O'odham, known for their beautiful basket weaving.

MID-MARCH

SCOTTSDALE, AZ
NATIONAL FESTIVAL OF THE WEST
(602) 996-4387

This large Western-themed event includes a mountain-man rendezvous that brings out would-be trappers and cowboys in costume.

MID-MARCH

TUCSON, AZ
WAK POW WOW
(520) 573-4000

The Tohono O'odham host this celebration of various Native American groups at San Xavier del Bac.

MID-MARCH

DENVER, CO
POWWOW
(303) 934-8045

One of the largest such events in the country, this powwow attracts more than seven hundred Native Americans from seventy tribes in a celebration of dance and craftsmanship.

MID-MARCH

ALBUQUERQUE, NM
RIO GRANDE ARTS AND CRAFTS FESTIVAL
Expo New Mexico
(505) 292-7457
www.riograndefestivals.com

Handcrafted works of more than two hundred artisans are featured in this annual event.

APRIL

ALBUQUERQUE, NM
GATHERING OF THE NATIONS POWWOW
(505) 836-2810

www.gatheringofnations.com

This annual event brings together crafts exhibitions, dance competitions, and Native American music.

MAY

5
VARIOUS LOCATIONS
CINCO DE MAYO

Cinco de Mayo has major celebrations in El Paso, TX; Las Cruces, NM; Los Angeles, CA; Phoenix, AZ; Santa Barbara, CA; and Tucson, AZ.

MID-MAY
SANTA MONICA, CA
SANTA MONICA INDIAN ART SHOW

Santa Monica Civic Auditorium

1855 Main Street

(310) 458-8551

www.americanindianartshow.com

This two-day event brings dealers of antique and contemporary Native American arts together under one roof.

LAST SATURDAY
JEMEZ PUEBLO, NM
JEMEZ RED ROCKS ARTS & CRAFTS SHOW

(505) 834-0103

This annual craft show features jewelry, weavings, pottery, and other wares along with a powwow and native foods.

JUNE

MID-JUNE
SANTA FE, NM
RODEO DE SANTA FE

(505) 471-4300

This multiday celebration features rodeo performances, dance, crafts exhibitions, and other Western-themed events.

MID-JUNE
SAN ANTONIO, TX
TEXAS FOLKLIFE FESTIVAL

Institute of Texan Cultures

(210) 458-2300

www.texasfolklifefestival.org

An arts and crafts market is the focal point of this celebration of food, music, and colorful costumes representing the various cultures of Texas.

JULY

4
FLAGSTAFF, AZ
*ANNUAL HOPI MARKETPLACE

Museum of Northern Arizona

(928) 774-5213

www.muznaz.org

This exhibition and sale showcases some of the best of Hopi craftsmanship.

4
PRESCOTT, AZ
PRESCOTT FRONTIER DAYS

(800) 358-1888

www.worldsoldestrodeo.com

Billed as the oldest rodeo in the United States, this event features rodeo competitions and showcases Western craftsmanship in saddles, spurs, boots, and hats.

9, 10, 11
TAOS PUEBLO
TAOS PUEBLO POWWOW

(505) 758-1028

Visitors can experience this important religious festival and shop for handmade pottery, jewelry, and other crafts.

SECOND WEEKEND
PRESCOTT, AZ
PRESCOTT INDIAN ART MARKET

Sharlot Hall Museum

(928) 445-3122

www.sharlot.org/events/indianart/

The Sharlot Hall Museum hosts an annual exhibition of Native American arts with an impressive number of craft demonstrations.

THIRD WEEKEND

TAOS PUEBLO, NM
FIESTAS DE SANTIAGO Y SANTA ANA
(800) 732-8267

Taos Pueblo hosts a series of celebrations of these patron saints, including dances, special masses, and craft exhibitions.

LAST WEEKEND

ALBUQUERQUE, NM
EXPO NEW MEXICO
New Mexico Arts & Crafts Fair
(505) 884-9043
www.nmartsandcraftsfair.org

Started in 1962, this showcase of the state's fine artists and craftspeople is one of the Southwest's longest running and largest celebrations.

LAST WEEKEND

SANTA FE, NM
*SPANISH MARKET
(505) 982-2226
www.spanishmarket.org

This is the Southwest's premier annual event for Hispanic craftspeople, held on the Plaza in Santa Fe. This is the best place to pick up santos, furniture, jewelry, wrought iron, and other crafts.

LATE JULY

BIG BEAR LAKE, CA
OLD MINERS' DAYS

This festival celebrates California's Gold Rush history with a variety of events.

AUGUST

EARLY AUGUST

COSTA MESA, CA
NATIVE AMERICAN POWWOW
(714) 962-6673

Native American food, dance, and crafts are featured in this annual festival.

EARLY AUGUST

SANTA BARBARA, CA
OLD SPANISH DAYS FIESTA
(805) 962-8101
www.oldspanishdays-fiesta.org

Dancing, music, Mexican food, and handcrafted items add to the colorful displays of this festival.

EARLY AUGUST

ALBUQUERQUE, NM
GREAT SOUTHWESTERN ANTIQUES,
INDIAN & OLD WEST SHOW
(505) 255-4054

The Great Southwestern Antiques, Indian & Old West Show showcases works from all three traditions, including some antiques, on the grounds of Expo New Mexico.

EARLY AUGUST

GALLUP, NM
INTER-TRIBAL INDIAN CEREMONIAL
(800) 242-4282
www.gallupnm.org

Crafts play a role in this celebration of many Native American tribes in various locations around Gallup.

MID-AUGUST

SANTA FE, NM
*SANTA FE INDIAN MARKET
(505) 983-5220
www.swaia.org/market.php

Similar to Santa Fe's famous Spanish Market, the Indian Market assembles more than twelve hundred craftspeople selling works representative of the major craft traditions of the Southwest.

THIRD WEEKEND

PRESCOTT, AZ
ARIZONA COWBOY POETS' GATHERING
(928) 445-3122
www.sharlot.org

Cowboy poets, storytellers, and other buckaroos take center stage at this festival of Western culture.

SEPTEMBER

EARLY SEPTEMBER

WINDOW ROCK, AZ
NAVAJO NATION FAIR

(928) 871-6478

www.navajonationfair.org

This large celebration highlights traditional
Navajo crafts, dancing, and traditional music.

EARLY SEPTEMBER

ALBUQUERQUE, NM
NEW MEXICO STATE FAIR

(505) 265-1791

www.nmstatefair.com

This traditional state fair features events from
rodeos to Native American dances, and exhibits
many of the time-proven crafts of all three traditions of the Southwest.

EARLY SEPTEMBER

SANTA FE, NM
LA FIESTA DE SANTA FE

(505) 988-7575

www.santafefiesta.org

This rowdy celebration has been entertaining
locals and visitors since 1712. Dances, masses,
parades, and craft demonstrations are included.

EARLY SEPTEMBER

TAOS, NM
NORTHERN NEW MEXICO CULTURAL
ART CELEBRATION

(505) 758-3873

This event features the work of both Hispanic
and Native American craftspeople.

SECOND FRIDAY

ROSWELL, NM
PINATAFEST CULTURAL CELEBRATION

(505) 624-0889

www.roswellhcc.com

This three-day celebration of Hispanic culture
and crafts is sponsored by the Roswell Hispanic
Chamber of Commerce.

MID-SEPTEMBER

SEDONA, AZ
FIESTA DEL TLAQUEPAQUE

Tlaquepaque Village

Held along the flower-bedecked streets and cor-
ridors of Sedona's premier craft-shopping district, this festival celebrates Hispanic and Native
American craftsmanship.

MID-SEPTEMBER

PAHRUMP, NV
PAHRUMP HARVEST FESTIVAL AND
RODEO

www.pahrumpharvestfestival.com

Cowboy craftsman join with rodeo stars, enter-
tainers, pit barbecuers, and more.

16

SANTA MONICA, CA
MEXICAN INDEPENDENCE DAY

Mexican dancing, food, and crafts celebrate
Mexican independence.

LATE SEPTEMBER

TAOS, NM
TAOS FALL ARTS & CRAFTS FAIR

Kit Carson Park

(505) 758-3873

One of the region's largest craft fairs showcases the work of hundreds of New Mexico artisans.

OCTOBER

EARLY OCTOBER

DURANGO, CO
COWBOY GATHERING

(970) 382-7494

www.durangocowboygathering.com

Nearly every aspect of cowboy culture is covered in some way at this annual event, including a display of Western craftsmanship.

EARLY OCTOBER

SHIPROCK, NM
SHIPROCK NAVAJO FAIR

(800) 448-1240

www.farmingtonnm.org

Crafts play a big part in this Navajo fair along with dancing, singing, and a rodeo.

NOVEMBER

I

VARIOUS LOCATIONS
EL DIA DE LOS MUERTOS (DAY OF THE DEAD)

Important celebrations take place in Mesa, AZ; Chandler, AZ; Guadalupe, AZ; Los Angeles, CA; San Antonio, TX; and San Diego, CA.

MID-NOVEMBER

PHOENIX, AZ
HEARD SPANISH MARKET

(602) 252-8848

www.heard.org

This relatively new event is already one of the region's best places to find Hispanic crafts from santos to tinware.

SECOND SATURDAY

FARMINGTON, NM
WOOL FESTIVAL OF THE SOUTHWEST

(505) 325-2837

www.woolfestivalsw.meridianI.net

This gathering of textile artisans includes demonstrations of sheepshearing and a tapestry auction.

DECEMBER

FIRST FULL WEEKEND

SANTA FE, NM
WINTER SPANISH MARKET

Sweeney Center

A wintertime version of the famous summer Spanish Market, this event assembles more than a hundred craftspeople selling wrought iron, santos, ceramics, and other Hispanic crafts.

MID-DECEMBER

PHOENIX, AZ
PUEBLO GRANDE MUSEUM INDIAN MARKET

Pueblo Grande Museum and Archaeological Park

(877) 706-4408

www.pgmarket.org

This is one of the largest gatherings of Native American artisans, representing more than sixty tribes from across the Southwest. You can buy pottery, jewelry, baskets, and other crafts directly from the artisans.

ABOUT THE AUTHOR

Laura Morelli is a writer and cultural historian with a passion for the world's craft traditions. Morelli holds a Ph.D. in art history from Yale University, as well as degrees in languages. She has taught at Trinity College, Tufts University, and Northeastern University, and has lectured to public audiences at the Museum of Fine Arts in Boston. A native of coastal Georgia, Morelli now lives in Connecticut with her family. Her book, *Made in Italy: A Shopper's Guide to Italy's Best Artisanal Traditions from Murano Glass to Ceramics, Jewelry, Leather Goods, and More*, was published by Universe in 2003.